SIMPLE, SMART
INVESTING

IAN KENNEDY

SIMPLE, SMART INVESTING

A How-To Investment Guide for Everyone

INKA PUBLISHING

ISBN 978-0-615-86906-3

10 9 8 7 6 5 4 3 2 1

Book design by Kim Adlerman

For Karla, with cause

Table of Contents

Part III: DON'T BELIEVE WHAT THEY TELL YOU ABOUT . . .

Part IV: CONSTRUCTING AND MANAGING AN INVESTMENT PORTFOLIO

Foreword

Ian Kennedy has been my "go to" guy for 22 years! Ian was head of research for Cambridge Associates, for many years the dominant investment consultant to universities, foundations, and wealthy families, the investors that have seen the most success during the last quarter century. I was the founding CEO of Stanford Management Company, and later the Chief Investment Officer of the Hewlett Foundation. He and I have had many lively debates!

I found Ian to be that rare consultant: both sides of his brain are engaged and highly active. He can give you left-brained, rigorous analysis. His right brain is on fire with well-considered views about how investors behave, both rationally and irrationally. This adds up to a complete package that has helped me enormously.

This book is, in turn, the complete package for individual investors. I've seen books that address some of the issues Ian goes after, but never one that not only addresses every issue important to the individual investor but also helps you decide which of these issues are crucial to *your* getting the outcome you want. He shows that he's not in love with his own words by telling you what parts of the book you need to read in your circumstances and which you can ignore.

Here are the other reasons you'll love this book:

• Ian writes in a breezy, conversational style. You'll think you and he are sitting in front of his fireplace talking as he helps you sort the wheat from the chaff about investing.

• He will walk you through an assessment of your understanding of investments, so you will know what you need to learn. He will then let you know which parts of the book you should read.

• He will tell you how to avoid being swept along by the emotions of the crowd.

• He will tell you the unvarnished truth about Wall Street's eagerness to charge you high fees, which may be transparent or hard-to-suss-out.

• He will coach you on how to write a simple investment policy to guide your program. In fact, he will *urge* you to write such a policy to remind you of your objectives so you can keep calm and focused during emotional times in the markets. This will steady you when you may be tempted to run for cover.

Best of all, he'll tell you when to shelve his book and put your plan into action. You will have a "win-win." Executing your plan will be simple; since it will be built around long term objectives, it will need little maintenance. Best of all, it will have high likelihood of success.

Let Ian Kennedy be your "go to" source for your personal investments. You'll make maximum progress with minimum effort. This book will ensure that your effort will be laser-focused on the right decisions.

Laurance (Laurie) Hoagland
Former CEO, Stanford Management Company
Former CIO, Wm. and Flora Hewlett Foundation
Woodside, California
August 2013

Preface

At the end of 2009, I retired from Cambridge Associates, a global investment consulting firm whose clients are institutional investors and very wealthy families.[i] For most of my 21 years there I was director of research, which meant that I spent a lot of time thinking and writing about the stock and bond markets. In its institutional practice, Cambridge Associates' particular focus is endowment funds, whether at colleges and universities, philanthropic foundations or countries' sovereign wealth funds.

And so I also thought and wrote a great deal about how our clients should invest. Not just what they should invest in, but how they should organize their decision-making to improve the odds of realizing their investment objectives. Also, what those objectives should be and how best to balance the trade-off between investment risk and investment returns.

Having retired, I naturally found myself spending more time with people *outside* the investment world. But they were also investors, since they were either retired, approaching retirement, or—like my children—trying to save towards their retirement. And when they learned my background, they would often ask me investment questions, like "what do you think the market will do this year?" or "where do you think interest rates are heading?"

I quickly realized I had two options: I could explain that volumes of research have shown the total unreliability of any such forecasts, no matter who makes them, or I could just say something like "as long as the Fed keeps rates this low, I don't see the market selling off too much." The first response just annoyed people and the second was pretty harmless, so I quickly opted for the latter.

But the more I ruminated on this, the more concerned I became that even highly intelligent and well-informed individuals seemed badly misinformed about what was and wasn't important when it came to investing. So I started paying more attention to their sources of information and quickly realized that it came, naturally enough, from the financial services industry. Like firms in any other industry, financial services firms try to make as much money as they can for management and shareholders. And of course the source of those earnings is their customers.

The problem here is that to make money, these firms typically encourage investors to think and act in ways that are very bad for their financial health. Most investors don't realize this is going on because they don't get a useful scorecard.

The end result is that savers earn less than they could, retirees have less money than they should, and the few people who raise their voices in protest are shouting into the wind.

And that's why I decided to write this book.

Acknowledgements

This project would have been dead in the water long ago had I not benefited from the editorial assistance and sage counsel of Susannah Harris, whose invaluable recommendations as to content, structure and format are reflected everywhere in this book.

Susannah also advised on the look and structure of my website, www.simplesmartinvesting.com, which was designed and built by Stephen Chovanec. Check it out—I think you'll agree he did an outstanding job!

Alex Jones at Cambridge Associates created all the exhibits and has been a terrific help with data. His patience through multiple cycles of updates and revisions has been exemplary and without his help there would be no book. I'd also like to thank Christina Fenton-Neblett of Cambridge Associates for her expert copyediting of all the exhibits.

I'm grateful to Laurie Hoagland for agreeing to write a foreword. For decades, Laurie has been a leading authority on endowment fund investing, having served as the President of Stanford Management Company and then Chief Investment

Officer of the Hewlett Foundation. His contributions to the endowment world are many and deep, and I've greatly valued both his wisdom and his friendship over the years.

Both my son, Alan, who knows very little about investing, and my colleague and friend, David Ingram, who knows a great deal, gave me excellent feedback at different stages of the writing.

Michael Jacobs and several of his colleagues at Abrams very kindly spent time advising me on publishing, about which I know nothing whatsoever.

Temma Ehrenfeld provided immaculate copy-editing, and encouragement, while Merrill Kaitz proofread the final copy.

From an aesthetic point of view, this is the work of Kim Adlerman, the book's designer, who has been a pleasure to work with—and the book looks great, doesn't it!?

Introduction

IS THIS BOOK NECESSARY?

It shouldn't be, because there are several excellent books already in circulation that cover much of the same ground and give similar advice. But on the other side of the deck there's an army of financial advisors who earn their living selling investors products and services that cost a lot but don't add a nickel of value. They can do so because most people simply don't know enough about investing to question the sales pitch. This book will tell you what you need to know and how to use your knowledge to invest wisely.

That's the plan. Here are the roadblocks:

First, will this book reach the millions of investors who need it? Probably not. Most people, even if they have money to invest, have better things to do with their time than plow through investment primers.

Secondly, like the authors listed in my "Recommended Reading" appendix, I'm going to bombard you with incontrovertible data disproving the falsehoods and delusions investors are constantly fed by financial-service firms charging high fees for inferior returns—and yet most of you will shrug and carry on as before. Faced with hard evidence disproving something we have long believed (e.g., my financial advisor can help me pick mutual funds that will outperform), we frequently dismiss the evidence and stick with what we think we know, as if somehow the data didn't apply to us.

So this book is a quixotic enterprise: its odds of reaching those who need it most are pretty slim, and even those it reaches may simply ignore the information and advice it provides because these require them to question popular assumptions, upset longstanding relationships, and change some rooted investment habits.

WHO IS THIS BOOK FOR?

It's for three kinds of investors, with anything from a few thousand dollars of savings to as much as $10 million:

Group One: Those who want to save and invest for their future, but know little or nothing about investing, don't have the time or inclination to learn, and just want to be told what to do. Read this introduction plus the first two chapters and you're done.

Group Two: Those who want to save and invest for their future, know little or nothing about investing, but are interested in learning more. Read the whole book (it's pretty short!) and browse the list of recommended books for further reading.

Group Three: Those who regard themselves as savvy and successful investors, like to play the markets, and are pretty sure they have an edge on the other punters out there. Frankly, you're probably beyond the pale, lost in delusions of superiority. But you should at least test your investment knowledge by honestly scoring yourself against the information in chapters four through 10, which document misconceptions many people have about investing. If you find that you didn't know most of what's here, then perhaps you're not as savvy as you imagine.

And how do you measure whether you've been successful? Individual investors typically overestimate both their investment acumen and their success rate. If you haven't kept score properly (see chapter 14, "Keeping Score"), you've probably done worse than you assume. And unless you keep score properly in the future, you'll never know whether your decisions are adding or detracting value.

Please Note: This isn't a book on financial planning

If you're looking for comprehensive financial-planning advice, I'm afraid you won't find it here.

There are excellent books on how to budget your spending, save for college tuition and retirement, manage tax liabilities, make prudent decisions on debt and insurance—and so on.

The only advice I can offer on financial planning is that if you seek professional help, you should be very careful and look up online resources that tell you what you need to learn about any financial planner before you hire one—just Google "what to ask a financial planner," and you'll find what you need.

It's particularly important that you learn how they get paid. As with investment advisors, you should generally avoid those whose income comes (in whole or in part) from commissions on products they sell.

WHAT'S IN THIS BOOK?

Part I: *Just Tell Me What to Do*

Chapter 1: Do It Yourself or Hire an Advisor?

As an investor, the first question you confront is whether you should go it alone or employ an investment advisor.

"Investment advisor" shouldn't be confused with "investment manager." An advisor's job is to draw up an investment plan, including how your money should be allocated among different investments and how the plan should be implemented, with this percentage invested in Fund A, this in Fund B—and so on. Then the advisor oversees your portfolio on an ongoing basis.

On the other hand, a manager is someone who manages a mutual fund or similar investment product.

The decision as to whether to hire an investment advisor should not be made on the basis of ego or gut instinct—do-it-yourselfers should meet certain minimum standards of knowledge, competence and commitment, otherwise they'll just shoot themselves in the foot. Chapter 1 suggests what these criteria should be.

Since many investors lack the knowledge, interest, time and temperament to manage their own portfolios effectively, the second part of this chapter gives detailed advice on selecting an investment advisor—what to look for and what to avoid.

Chapter 2: How to Go It Alone

This chapter is for those who really aren't interested in investing, but don't want to hire an advisor or haven't built up sufficient savings to warrant doing so. But you have to do *something*, right? Perhaps money is piling up in your 401(k), you're funding an IRA every year, and you're smart enough to realize you need additional long-term savings for retirement. "Just tell me what to do!" is your plaintive cry.

Okay.

Chapter 2 will minimize your need to do much of anything, after you've spent a little time and energy setting everything in motion. Read the chapter, follow the plan, shelve the book.

Part II: *The Capital Markets*

Chapter 3

In a capitalist society, the capital markets are the mechanism through which investors' savings are channeled into the economy, funding public and private companies, and local, state and federal government debt. Just as a vegetable market is a forum for the buying and selling of vegetables, so the capital markets are forums for the buying and selling of stocks, bonds and other investable assets—like precious metals or mortgage-backed securities.

All investors should have some understanding of how this mechanism works and a modicum of knowledge about the history of capital markets. This is the foundation on which investment decisions should be built.

So chapter 3 gives a brief account of US capital markets history, focusing on the relative risk and return of equities (*aka* stocks), bonds and cash since 1900. These sections are followed by primers on equities and equity investing and on bonds and bond investing.

Part III: *Don't Believe What They Tell You About . . .*

Chapters 4 to 11

No sector of the economy stimulates such a torrent of information, news, commentary, advice, advertising and product sales as the financial services sector. What other industry has entire newspapers and TV channels devoted to its coverage 24/7? Unfortunately, much of this bombardment is, at best, irrelevant and, at worst, profoundly misleading.

So chapters 4 through 11 briefly address some of the more common misconceptions fed to investors and provide antidotes to combat their toxic effects.

In addition, they serve as a reality check for readers who think they already know the ropes; if a good deal of what's covered in these chapters is news, perhaps you still have some way to go.

Part IV: *Constructing and Managing an Investment Portfolio*

If you want to manage your own investments, you'd better be equipped. This means you should:

- Digest the material about the capital markets in chapter 3.

- Understand how to construct an investment portfolio designed to realize your objectives.

- Recognize what risks you're exposing your money to and how to manage those risks.

- Measure your results against suitable yardsticks so that you can tell how well you're doing.

None of which is simple and obvious. So the chapters in this section are more demanding, but should be especially interesting to those who really want to learn about investing.

Chapter 12: Investment Planning and Asset Allocation

All investors, whether going it alone or using an advisor, should have a coherent *written* investment plan that clearly states where they're going and how they intend to get there.

xxvi / Simple Smart Investing

Such a plan need not be long, but it should include:

- The purposes for which you are investing.

- How much money you hope to accumulate.

- When you hope to get there.

- Your savings plan.

- How you intend to allocate your investment assets among different kinds of investments (e.g., stocks and bonds).

- How you will implement those allocations; that is, which stocks, bonds, mutual funds or exchange-traded funds (ETFs) you will choose.

- An acknowledgement of the risks you'll incur along the way.

- A commitment to rebalance the asset mix of your total investment portfolio back to the target allocations mapped out in your policy statement. This can be done by redirecting savings into whichever asset class[ii] has gone down in value, or by selling some of the assets that have gone up in value and using the proceeds to buy more of those that have gone down.

Without such a map, your journey will be aimless and your route filled with expensive and unnecessary detours. This is all covered in chapter 12.

Chapter 13: Risk and Risk Management

Even relatively sophisticated investors often don't know how to define their risk tolerance. Moreover, books about investing typically treat risk as a single, invariant attribute of the investment process.

In fact, when it comes to risk, we're often our own worst enemy. When the stock market is booming, we're elated and confident, focused on the great returns we're earning and oblivious to risk. When markets tank, our risk tolerance quickly shrinks and we watch anxiously as our portfolio value shrivels. Of course, this is the wrong way around: when markets boom, risk is rising; when they crash, risk diminishes. But that's not how we *feel*.

So risk is discussed here in both traditional and behavioral terms. That is, both in terms of the probability of suffering a loss of x% over a period of y years or of not having the money you need when you need it, and also in terms of our emotional response to market events.

However, identifying the various risks incurred by investors isn't much help unless we also understand how these can be monitored and managed. So that's covered in the second half of this chapter.

Chapter 14: Keeping Score

If you don't keep score properly, how do you know if you're winning or losing? Unfortunately, most mutual fund and brokerage firm statements give you only one score: whether you have more or less money in your account than you had last quarter and at the beginning of the year. This is necessary information, but far from sufficient, and so you're going to have to set up your own scorecard to tell how you're doing.

Here you'll learn what the scorecard should include and how it should be constructed and maintained.

Conclusion

Like any conclusion, mine attempts to wrap everything up and hammer home the book's main points.

Appendices

There are three of these at the end of the book:

• A sample letter to your company's HR department recommending changes to your company's 401(k) plan. Unless your 401(k) plan is already with a firm that offers low-cost index funds (e.g., Fidelity, Schwab, TIAA-CREF or Vanguard), you should probably be lobbying your firm to switch to one of those so that you can have access to such funds as an investment option.

• A glossary of investment terms. It would really clunk up the text if I stopped to define every investment term used along the way. Instead, you can turn to the glossary whenever you come across a term you don't know.

• An annotated list of recommended further reading.

Indexes

In standard terminology, an index is simply a listing—usually alphabetical—of names or titles or subjects mentioned in a book.

In the investment world, however, an index is a basket of stocks or bonds or any other investable assets (e.g., commercial real estate), the returns of which are used as an indicator of the returns for that sector of the investment markets.

For example, the best-known US stock market index is the Dow Jones Industrial Average (DJIA), consisting of the shares of 30 large industrial companies, each assigned a different weight. Their returns are intended as a kind of proxy for the returns of all major US industrial companies' shares.

A rather better representation of the US stock market is the S&P 500 Index, consisting of 500 US companies, chosen by a committee nominated by Standard and Poor's, which is weighted by market capitalization.[iii] In other words, if Company A's stock market value is $50 billion and Company B's is $25 billion, then A's returns have twice as much weight in the index as B's.

However, the S&P 500 actually represents only the largest 85% of the US stock market.

Indexes that capture closer to 100% of the market include the Russell 3000, a capitalization-weighted index of the largest 3000 stocks in the market, and the Wilshire 5000, which—despite its name—includes only 3,563 stocks, but nevertheless covers virtually the whole US stock market, excluding only the most tiny issues.

There are also stock indexes targeted at specific segments of the market; for example, the Russell 1000 Index is a subset of the Russell 3000 that includes the largest 1,000 US companies, while the Russell 2000 Index covers the smallest two-thirds of companies in the Russell 3000.

Similarly, there are indexes representing different economic segments of the market, like energy companies, health-care companies, or real estate investment trusts. And there are indexes consisting of companies that share certain characteristics, like a large dividend payout, or rapid earnings growth. There are also indexes composed of non-US stocks and bonds, whether across entire regions (e.g., Europe) or one country (e.g., Turkey).

In short, nowadays you can find an index representing almost any sector, segment or market characteristic you could think of. And all of those indexes are now investable, through mutual funds or exchange-traded funds (ETFs).[iv]

Bond indexes follow the same script. That is, there is a bond index, the Barclay's Aggregate Bond Index, that aspires to represent the entire US bond market (excluding tax-free municipal bonds), and has sub-sectors representing segments of the bond market, such as corporate bonds, government agency bonds, Treasury bonds, and others.

Indexing

Indexing is the practice of buying shares in a fund that invests in a particular index. The term "passive investing" is often used as a synonym for indexing because the essence of indexing is that you are not paying someone to pick stocks, or decide if it would be better to own utility companies rather than drug companies, and so on. That is called "active investing" because instead of simply owning all the shares included in a given index, the fund manager is making "active" decisions about what stocks to own and not own, what stocks to own more of and less of, and so on (see later chapters on active and passive investing).

There are two reasons why investors put their money into index funds rather than actively managed funds.

- The first is that reams of research over many decades has shown that most actively managed US stock funds have consistently failed to produce better returns than investors could have earned in an index fund comprising the full basket of stocks from which the managers are selecting stocks.

- In fact, over almost every time period studied, two-thirds of actively managed funds have earned *worse* returns than those of a relevant index fund.

• Although this means that one-third of actively managed funds have outperformed index funds, no one has figured out how to identify which funds will outperform in the future (although we have figured out that they generally won't be those that outperformed in the past).

• The second reason to invest in index funds is that they cost much less than actively managed funds, which gives them a huge advantage over the long term, since small amounts compounded over time add up to very large amounts in the end (see chapter 11, "Costs Matter Far More Than You Think").

A common criticism of indexing is that since most stock market indexes are capitalization-weighted, investors own more and more of whatever stocks have gone up in price the most, and less and less of those that have lagged. Why should this be a problem? Well, multiple research studies have shown that on average the shares of companies investors don't much like and don't value very highly have generated better returns over time than those of companies everyone loves and admires.[v] And so if you invest in a capitalization-weighted index you're obviously going to own more shares of those companies everyone loves than of those everyone ignores or dislikes.

But it's easy to counter this effect: you can simply tilt your investments towards so-called value indexes (e.g., the Russell

1000 Value Index) that are more heavily weighted in companies investors don't value so highly. Or you can look into "fundamental indexes" (e.g., at Charles Schwab), which weight companies by factors other than market capitalization. Or you could choose an index fund that equally weights its component stocks, which will result in a strong tilt to smaller-capitalization issues.

But you should realize that if you go down such roads, you're making more and more "active" decisions and moving further away from purely "passive" investing, since the most passive investment you can make is simply to buy into the whole US market through a fund like the Vanguard Total Stock Market Index Fund. Then your investment dollars will be allocated among all the stocks in the market in exactly the same proportions as the aggregate investment dollars of all other investors.

Part I

JUST TELL ME WHAT TO DO

CHAPTER 1

Do It Yourself or Hire an Advisor?

HOW SHOULD YOU DECIDE?

If you don't have the time, interest or temperament to manage your own investment assets properly, you should hand the job over to a competent professional. Their services don't come cheap, but in the long run will prove a huge bargain compared to the botched job you'll do on your own or by entrusting yourself to the tender mercies of most "advisors" employed by banks, brokers or insurance companies.

Research by the consulting firm Aon Hewitt and the investment advisor Financial Engines covering 425,000 savers during the period 2006 to 2010 revealed that "the median annual return of those who got professional help was almost three percentage points higher than the return for those who invested on their own," even after fees."[vi]

This isn't surprising. If we're not lawyers, we're at a severe disadvantage if we represent ourselves in a lawsuit. If we have no training in finance, we're not likely to shine as a company's CFO. Yet we get bombarded daily with the message that we're perfectly capable of "winning" in the investment arena. How come? Simple: there's a huge and highly profitable industry that sells this delusion because it gets well paid for doing so.

I used the word "arena" deliberately. Many attributes of investing involve combat—your gain is someone else's loss. And the stakes are often very high. Even highly experienced, professional, institutional investors periodically crash and burn despite their numerous advantages over individuals like you and me. First, their costs are lower—and over time that's a huge comparative advantage (see chapter 11, "Costs Matter Far More Than You Think"). Secondly, they have superior access to valuable information (I can't afford a Bloomberg terminal at home, can you?). Thirdly, this is what they do all day, every day, so they should possess a level of knowledge, experience and expertise others don't. Finally, they measure their performance against suitable yardsticks, which tells them whether, how, why and when they or the managers they hire are adding value. This feedback informs their subsequent decision-making.

Can you compete against all that? I can't. In fact, it's because I spent 20 plus years advising institutional investors, and still serve on the investment committees of several multi-billion dollar endowment funds, that I see how badly the playing field is biased against the individual investor.

Institutions aren't different from us just because they have more money; they're different because they have far greater resources, particularly expertise, that give them the same advantage an experienced lawyer has in a legal battle with a self-taught amateur.

So how expert are you? If you answer "no" or "not really" to most of the following questions, you're probably better off outsourcing the management of your investments to a qualified professional:

- Are you interested in investing?

- Do you have enough time or will you make time to learn more about investing?

- Are you a regular and disciplined saver?

- Do you have, or will you commit to developing, a written investment plan that integrates your financial circumstances and goals with your investment objectives?

- Is the asset allocation of your investment portfolio aligned with your investment objectives and time horizon?

- Do you understand investment risk and know how to assess and manage your own risk tolerance?

- Do you rebalance your portfolio to maintain your chosen asset allocation?

- Do you keep track of your investment performance, net of all fees, expenses and taxes?

• Do you measure your portfolio's performance against that of a paper portfolio with the same asset allocation as yours, but composed of relevant stock and bond market indexes?

These are minimum requirements for you to manage your own investments. So be honest—how many "yes" answers did you give? And if you answered "no" to some, do you have the interest—and the time—to turn them into "yes"?

If you answer "yes" to these next three questions, you should perhaps think about whether you are temperamentally equipped to manage your own money:

• Are you susceptible to ads or sales pitches for investment products promising outsize returns, or good returns with no downside risk?

• Are you likely to invest in a mutual fund because it has a great three-year record?

• When the stock market plummets, as it did in 2008-09, do you dump your equity investments to protect your portfolio against further declines?

Finally, what about your family, if you have one? If you're hit by the proverbial bus, is your spouse competent to take over? Or should you put in place a plan that ensures the assets will be capably handled by your professional advisor?

A warning, however, to those who decide someone else should oversee their money: no matter how little you're interested in the subject of investing, you must devote the necessary time and effort to identifying the right kind of investment advisor, or you'll put your life's savings at risk. The good news is that once you invest time up front, the ongoing demands should be light—which is exactly what you're paying for.

HOW TO HIRE THE RIGHT INVESTMENT ADVISOR

When we know little or nothing about something that's important to us, we naturally feel somewhat intimidated by experts. We become susceptible to whatever they recommend—after all, they're in the know and we're not.

This is particularly true in the financial realm, where we're scared to make mistakes and are reassured by any professional guide who radiates conviction and authority. Investing is a profession, like medicine or law or accounting. Unfortunately, there are no laws setting minimum standards for education, experience, or expertise among those offering investment advice. As a result, most so-called "financial advisers" or "investment advisors"[vii] are simply salesmen whose job is to make the most money possible from you, not for you (as Charley Ellis puts it[viii]).

In this system, the "financial advisors" are on the prowl for new customers to whom they can sell their products and services. That's the wrong way round: you need to be the one finding and hiring the right investment advisor for you.

The rest of this chapter will tell you what kind of advisor to look for, where to look, what information you need to gather, where to find that information, what questions to ask those whom you interview, and how to arrive at a decision.

So, yes, hiring the right advisor takes some work. And there's a catch: most suitable investment advisors have what the industry calls "minimums." These might be as little as $50,000, but are often much higher—for example, $250,000 or even $1 million. Advisors are generally paid a percentage of "assets under management," the amount clients give them to invest, and so it's not worth their time to take on clients with smaller amounts.

If you haven't yet accumulated sufficient savings to qualify as a client for the advisor you think is right, either follow the advice in chapter two until you get there or else employ one of the two online advisory firms cited later in this chapter.

Sorting Out Investment Advisors

When you hire an investment advisor, you're essentially entering into a partnership; as with any partnership, you should be seeking to maximize alignment of interests and minimize conflicts of interest between you and your partner (by the way, this is also good marriage advice!).

With that in mind, here's what amounts to a checklist of what you want and don't want in an investment advisor.

The Kind of Advisors to Avoid

Let's first narrow the field by eliminating the undesirables.

You **DON'T** want anyone who:

• Works for a bank, insurance company, brokerage firm, or other large diversified financial services company. Their primary responsibility is to make money for the company and its shareholders, not for you. Your costs will be high and your investment returns relatively low. That's not an appealing combination!

• Is not personally a registered investment advisor (stockbrokers and insurance salesmen are not registered investment advisors, which means they have no fiduciary responsibility to their customers).

• Has violated securities laws and regulations.[ix]

• Earns commissions on products sold to you or anyone else.

• Charges a "wrap" fee for managing your account (see glossary).

• Plans to invest some of your money in so-called "structured products" (see glossary), which technically do not have fees attached, but are nevertheless extremely lucrative for the seller and potentially toxic for the investor. Most annuity products fall into this category.

• Plans to invest some of your money in hedge funds, with commodity trading advisors (CTAs), or in private investments of any sort (e.g., real estate, oil & gas partnerships, venture capital, or buyout funds). These kinds of investments are suitable only for highly sophisticated investors (most of whom still don't earn decent returns from investing in such areas) and if you're reading this book, well, sorry, that ain't you!

• Plans to invest most of your money in actively managed mutual funds (or separate accounts) as opposed to passive index funds. Some actively managed funds might be okay for some of your money (for example, there aren't viable index funds for investing in tax-free municipal bonds). However, most of your money should be invested in low-cost, passively managed index funds.

• Is primarily a financial planner rather than an investment advisor. Many financial planners (who should have the Certified Financial Planner [CFP] designation) can tell you whether an adjustable or fixed-rate mortgage would be better for you, or whether you'd do better leasing rather than buying a car, but still may be clueless about investing. Some financial planners also have investment knowledge and expertise, but this is not a given.

You might be surprised to learn that almost all of the trillions of dollars in millions of individual investors' accounts are managed by firms eliminated in this short checklist of no-nos. Gone are UBS, Wells Fargo, Bank of America Merrill Lynch, Citicorp, Goldman Sachs, J.P. Morgan, Morgan Stanley, Ameriprise Financial, and BNY Mellon; and a host of lesser banks, insurance companies, and mutual fund complexes. Gone also are thousands of small firms across America whose financial planning advice leads to the sale of commission-paying insurance and investment products to their clients. I'm afraid you'll have to read the whole book to understand why this is so.

Wealth Management Firms

In particular, investors with substantial financial assets (i.e., in excess of $1 million) are the target of commercial and investment banks' "wealth management" divisions. Surprisingly, information from such firms on basic issues like their fees and performance record are remarkably hard to come by.

In fact, a recent analysis by a Swiss-based research firm called MyPrivateBanking found that none of the large US wealth management firms provided such rudimentary data on their websites. Moreover, "even when clients extract performance and fee data from their managers, it's often difficult to fairly compare them to the market."[x]

As with most actively managed mutual funds, such firms attempt to steer prospects and clients away from any such comparisons because these would typically reveal an inability to add consistent value (net of fees, expenses, and taxes) relative to low-cost, passive investment alternatives.

Fraud

Of course, virtually all investors, from small savers to the very wealthy, are also vulnerable to outright fraud. The *Economist* magazine recently reported that a consulting firm had "identified more than 300 sizable Ponzi schemes from the past ten years, with combined losses for investors of $23 billion."

About half of these scams were "affinity-based," which means that investors entrusted their money to someone affiliated with their church or community. That is, they knew the fraudster personally or invested on the basis of a recommendation from a friend or associate.

If you follow the steps outlined below, you'll insulate yourself from such scams. If you invest with so-and-so just because he seems like an honest and knowledgeable person and was recommended by your neighbor, you're on your own.

The Kind of Advisors to Consider

What you **DO** want is someone who:

• Is independent. That is, has no financial incentive to invest your money in this product rather than that one.

• Is compensated by fees charged on assets under management. This means that the better your portfolio performs, the more money your advisor earns. That's what I mean by alignment of interest! The fee should never exceed 1.25% of assets, and should be tiered, meaning that it declines as you reach breakpoints. For example, the firm might charge 1.25% on the first $250,000 in assets, 1.0% on the next $250,000 to $500,000, 0.8% on the next $500,000 to $1 million, 0.6% on the next million, and so on. Many firms will also offer hourly fees and annual retainer fees for financial planning services.

• Is primarily an investment advisor (who may also provide some financial planning services), as opposed to primarily a financial advisor (who may also provide some investment advisory services).

• Can give you a clear description of their approach to investing. At a minimum, they should stress the following:

1. The development of a coherent investment plan written down in the form of an investment policy statement that is integrated with your unique financial goals, circumstances, and risk tolerance.[xi]

2. This statement should summarize what you are investing for (your investment objectives) and when you will need the money (your investment time horizon). It should also state how your savings will be allocated among different kinds of investments (e.g., stocks and bonds) in accordance with that time horizon and those objectives, and comment on the risk tolerance this entails.

3. The kind of investment products to be used in implementing the asset allocation plan. These need not necessarily be passive index funds only, but should cer-

tainly include index funds (particularly in taxable accounts), and should otherwise be transparent, no-load, and relatively low-cost funds. Any advisors using actively managed funds should justify their choices and make a compelling case that they have added value for their clients by doing so. In other words, indexing should be the default option.

4. A policy of rebalancing the mix of different investments to ensure that your actual asset allocation remains relatively close to the asset allocation mapped out in your investment policy statement.

5. An understanding of your tax situation and a focus on *after-tax* returns.

6. A regular review of your portfolio's risk and return, both in absolute terms and relative to appropriate market index benchmarks.

Does size matter?

Yes and no.

On the one hand, a firm consisting of one professional plus an administrative assistant can outsource certain operations to a firm like BAM or Loring Ward (see below) and provide highly personal service, effectively.

The problem here is what's called "key man" risk; that is, what if your advisor is hit by the proverbial bus, is consumed by a messy divorce, or contracts a debilitating disease? Who steps into the void to keep everything on course?

At larger firms, of course, there would be somebody to fill the void. Larger firms may also benefit from a diversity of perspectives offered by members of a team. But the larger the firm, the greater the chance that you'll be a speck on their map, as it were, although a good client- relationship manager can obviously help.[xii]

Moreover, very large investment advisors generally employ active managers, either selecting outside firms (e.g., Northern Trust) or employing their own (e.g., Bernstein Global Wealth Management), whereas most of your assets should be invested predominantly in passive index funds. For this reason alone, you should avoid larger firms serving thousands of clients in favor of somewhat smaller outfits whose investment strategy emphasizes index fund investing.

HOW TO COMPILE A SHORT LIST OF PROSPECTIVE INVESTMENT ADVISORS

Googling "fee-only investment advisors" doesn't work. When I did this, it generated brokerage firms touting their wrap fee programs; and wealth management firms that charged as much as 2.5% on assets under management, earned backdoor commissions from mutual funds levying the notorious 12b-1 fee, and garnered additional income from re-ferring clients to other service providers. No, no, and no. Absolutely not!

I realize that almost every writer on this subject suggests that you follow the time-honored route of asking your friends and associates if they know anyone they'd recommend. Sorry, but I can't go along with this advice. Why? Well, very few people—especially men—are willing to admit they're clueless about investing. So, yes, if they have any investments at all they'll probably recommend whomever they've been dealing with themselves. And this is probably a highly personable "financial advisor" or "investment consultant" at Raymond James or Merrill Lynch with whom they are very comfortable—but in fact they don't actually know what this arrangement costs them nor how their investments have performed compared to the performance of passive index funds that should be used as performance yardsticks.

So any such recommendations should be subjected to exactly the same scrutiny as all other potential advisors.

Here are five suggestions to help you identify fee-based investment advisors in your area that will invest your money predominantly in index funds:

• The website www.bamadvisorservices.com will enable you to locate fee-only investment advisors in your area that use this firm (BAM Advisor Services) as their operations manager, providing custody services, research, administrative support, performance reporting, and other back office functions. All the advisors in this network invest most of their clients' equity assets in enhanced index funds managed by Dimensional Fund Advisors (DFA), whose retail mutual funds are accessible only through fee-based financial planning and investment advisory firms.

• BAM Advisor Services is an offshoot of an investment advisory firm, Buckingham Asset Management, which you can hire as your money manager. Although Buckingham is based in St. Louis, the advisors it employs cover every state, so you can meet with an advisor in person on a regular basis. Buckingham's minimum fee is $5,000, however, so this is an expensive option for anyone with less than $400,000 in investable assets.

• Another company, Loring Ward (www.loringward.com), supports a similar network of financial and investment advisors, providing them with turnkey investment management services, again investing in DFA index funds. They will also e-mail you a list of local investment advisory firms they support.

• DFA itself will e-mail you a list of fee-based firms in your area that invest client assets in its funds. Just click on the "Individual Investor" section of its website (www.dfaus.com).

• Although relatively new and still not entirely reliable or comprehensive, www.BrightScope.com aspires to serve as a search tool for investors looking for financial or investment advisors meeting selected criteria (e.g., fee-based only firms in Indiana). Worth checking out.

Most people want to be able to sit down with their investment advisor in person, but if this doesn't matter to you here are four additional suggestions that will save you money; their fees are significantly lower:

• Portfolio Solutions (www.portfoliosolutions.com) provides low-cost investment management implemented through index funds and ETFs (exchange-traded funds). Note that it recommends a minimum account size of $1,000,000, although they will take smaller accounts. Fees are 0.37% on the first $3 million of assets, and 0.20% on assets in excess of $3 million.

• Similarly, Vanguard Asset Management Services offers relatively low-cost personalized account management for those with investable assets of $500,000 or more, with a minimum annual fee of $4,500. Vanguard's fee is 0.7% on the first million in assets, 0.35% on the next million, and 0.20% on additional amounts.

• Wealthfront.com and Betterment.com are online advisors that rely on academically rigorous formulae to determine the optimum asset allocation for your circumstances. Then they implement the asset allocation using low-cost index funds and ETFs, rebalancing back to the target allocations as necessary.

Of the two, Wealthfront.com offers a wider array of asset classes and emphasizes that it manages accounts as tax-efficiently as possible; for example, by realizing capital losses in order to offset capital gains.

Fees: Betterment.com charges 0.35% on accounts with assets up to $10,000, 0.25% on amounts between $10,000 and $100,000, and 0.15% on amounts over that. Wealthfront.com charges nothing on amounts up to $10,000 and 0.25% on assets in excess of $10,000.

The great appeal of both these firms is their willingness to manage relatively small amounts for very reasonable fees, and invest in low-cost index funds.

Whether you choose a face-to-face local advisor or go with a more impersonal online firm, you should question the assumptions underlying the asset allocation recommended for you. For example, if the assumption for the bond allocation is simply an extrapolation of the long-term average bond market return, you should question how anyone can possibly expect to realize this kind of return starting from a point in time (e.g., mid-2013) when bond yields are at unprecedented lows.

In other words, you should draw on the information in Chapter 3 to become an informed participant in the most important decision: your target asset allocation. Ask yourself whether the recommendations are influenced by a thoughtful analysis of your circumstances and objectives, or only the output of a computer model.

There are probably other places to search for independent, fee-only, qualified investment advisors—use your initiative!

However, even these few suggestions should give you a decent short list.

How to Gather Information on Prospective Investment Advisors

Having created a short list of potential advisors, you need to do some homework. Your assigned reading is on www.adviserinfo.sec.gov.

As noted above, any person or firm that receives compensation for investment advisory services must register with the Securities and Exchange Commission (SEC) or their state regulator, hence the term "registered investment adviser." Note that stockbrokers and other representatives of broker-dealer firms are not required to register with the SEC; they are considered sales people, not advisors (regardless of the title on their business cards).[xiii]

This is an important distinction that should raise a red flag: you do not want to entrust your hard-earned savings to people who derive their income from selling products or wrap-account fees.

In the left-hand column of the opening page of www.adviserinfo.sec.gov, click on "Investment Adviser Search." This will give you access to any firm's Form ADV, which contains a wealth of useful information. It's very easy to navigate and although much of the material is boilerplate stuff like the firm's address and office hours, you should pay particular attention to certain sections. See the appendix to this chapter, "What to Learn from an Investment Advisor's ADV," for a checklist to help narrow the field of prospective advisors.

Among other key questions, the ADV information solves the tricky issue of whether a firm is really a financial planning outfit or an investment advisory firm. Here's how to tell the difference:

Go to Items 5F (1 and 2) and 5G in the ADV. These questions ask:

- 5F (1): "Do you provide continuous and regular supervisory or management services to securities portfolios?"

- 5F (2): "If yes, what is the amount of your assets under management and total number of accounts?"

- 5G: What type(s) of advisory services do you provide. Check all that apply.

If 5F(1) is not checked (and therefore 5F(2) is blank) and 5G(2) is also not checked, this firm is not really in the investment advisory business. It might well give clients investment advice and sell them investment products, but it is not an investment advisor you want to manage your money.

HOW TO INTERVIEW PROSPECTIVE INVESTMENT ADVISORS

I said earlier that we're often intimidated by the expertise of others. But if you've followed the process outlined in this chapter, there's no reason to feel intimidated. Even if you don't know much about investing, you now know a great deal about the investment advisory firms you're going to interview. In fact, they'll be bowled over by how thoroughly you've prepared.

When you first contact a firm to arrange a time to visit, the receptionist will probably ask you to bring in financial statements, past tax returns, and so on. Just murmur something in response and then ignore this. You are interviewing them, not vice-versa.

Make this clear as soon as your meeting starts. If the person you sit down with starts asking you for financial information (and he or she probably will), politely respond that you're interviewing several firms you think might meet your needs and will happily provide all the necessary financial information to the firm you select. Say that you've read the firm's ADV and have several questions you'd like to ask. It's a good idea to confirm some of the details in the ADV.

- For example, ask first for the minimum account size and fees, as they might have changed since the firm updated the form.

- What size is the average client account? Also, what is the range of account sizes across all the firm's clients?

- Beyond the advisory fee, there may be transaction or administrative costs, fund expenses, and more. Ask for all costs. Everything. I cannot stress enough how much costs matter in the long run. After all, with some time and effort you could do it yourself, at all-in costs of less than 50 basis points (0.5%), so you must make sure you're getting value for the additional money you'll be spending.

• How many clients does the firm have? How many new clients has it added in the past 12 months and how many clients has it lost? Why did those clients leave?

• If the ADV indicates that some of the firm's revenues are from sources other than fees on the assets they manage for clients, ask for details on where those revenues come from.

• Similarly, ask if the firm has other businesses, such as estate planning or insurance services. You want to make sure that the firm concentrates on investment management.

• How do they ensure that accounts are managed in a tax-efficient way?

• When a new client signs up, what happens next? As I noted above, look for advisors who can give a clear account of their approach to investing. The list on page 14-15 is pretty much what you should hear when you ask what steps the firm follows with new clients.

• Can you see a sample of a client's quarterly report? If not, what do such reports include? The answer should be: some commentary on the markets and an account of any changes made in the composition of the client's portfolio. Returns should be reported for the quarter just ended, year-to-date, trailing 12 months, the past three and five years, and since inception of the account. These returns should be shown for the portfolio as a whole, for each asset class, and for each investment product. In every case, they should be paired with the returns for an appropriate benchmark index (e.g., the S&P 500 for US stocks).

• How often do the firm's representatives meet with each client?

• Ask for client references. When you contact them, ask what they like and dislike about the firm and the individual they consult with.

How to Arrive at a Decision

Your short list may have included perhaps five or six firms. Information on the ADV forms should rule out a few candidates. When you interview the remaining firms, you'll probably feel more comfortable with one than with the others. Any firm where the people act as if meeting with you is a massive favor should obviously be dumped immediately. But don't be dazzled by charm. You want someone who is patient and steady, and good with numbers—maybe even a bit dull. Charm is not a requirement!

If you do your homework properly and control the interviews, you won't have much trouble coming to a sensible conclusion.

CONCLUSION: WHO IS MY ADVISOR WORKING FOR?

In any relationship, there will be some conflict of interests. The only way to eliminate conflict is to go it alone.

But if you decide you'd be better off with an advisor, you need to know whether your advisor is really working for you or the firm and whether the firm is most interested in its clients or its owners or shareholders.

Your financial health is critically dependent on ensuring that the people you work with have powerful incentives to maximize your after-tax investment returns (with suitable risk controls), not their own compensation or their firm's profits. Far too many investors are cavalier or ignorant about what they pay for investment advice or management services and how they pay it.

Keeping a tight rein on costs is key to realizing your investment goals—for proof, see the math in chapter 11, "Costs Matter Far More Than You Think."

Consider two spouses who have each invested a cumulative total of $720,000 in monthly increments over 30 years, earning identical gross returns (i.e., before fees). However, one spouse has incurred annual fees of 0.2% and the other 1.2%. After 30 years, the first account will be $450,000 richer than the second. Yes, you read that correctly—that 1% fee differential, compounded over the years, amounts to $450,000. Now tell me investment expenses don't matter!

The kind of investment advisors I recommend do charge what may seem to be very high fees. It's also true that once your funds are properly invested, their job becomes pretty simple: they should invest your annual savings according to the long-term plan and rebalance your portfolio to maintain the proper asset allocation. As your portfolio appreciates, the dollar value of their fee will increase.

So is the firm worth an annual fee of 1% or so? Yes. I do think the average fee is too high, but that's the going rate, and frankly most of you will be far better off paying someone this fee than trying to manage your investments yourself. Remember the research showing that investors using advisors earned far better returns—three percentage points annually, even after fees—than those who managed their own portfolios. That's a huge incremental difference over time.

Finally, there is a middle course: you could pay a fee-based advisor to help you draw up a coherent investment plan and give you sound advice on which index funds might serve you best. Then you could implement the plan yourself and perhaps go back once a year for an annual checkup, paying a fee for each visit. However, you should only go this route if you're sure you have the discipline to institute a regular savings regimen, and the stomach to rebalance your asset allocation come hell or high water. Or you could read on, and by doing so perhaps acquire just enough knowledge to create and implement your own plan.

SUMMARY

If you've decided you should hire an investment advisor, you have three options:

1. Online service (Betterment.com, Wealthfront.com).

> Pros:
> - Low-cost
> - Small minimum account size
> - Investment plan implemented via low-cost index funds and ETFs
>
> Cons:
> - Impersonal
> - No local contact to sit down with

2. National firm (Portfolio Solutions, Vanguard)

> Pros:
> - Low-cost
> - Personalized service
> - Investment plan implemented via low-cost index funds and ETFs
>
> Cons:
> - No local contact to sit down with

3. Local firm (sourced by e-mailing BAM, Loring Ward, and DFA)

Pros:

- Personalized service
- Investment plan implemented mostly via low-cost index funds and ETFs
- Face-to-face meetings with local firm

Cons:

- Higher cost
- More intensive due diligence required

APPENDIX

What to Learn from an Investment Advisor's ADV

Form ADV is a well-organized document divided into "items" that each deal with a different topic. For example, Item 1 asks for basic identification information: the firm's name, location, telephone number, hours of business, and so on.

When researching a firm, you should read through the whole ADV; however, here are the items you should pay close attention to. **I have indicated in bold those that are critical:**

Item 2A: The firm should have assets under management of $25 million or more; otherwise it's a barely sustainable enterprise and you run the risk that it will go under.

Item 2B: Is the firm registered to do business in your state of residence? Most states don't require firms to register for fewer than, say, five, clients in that state. So even if the answer is no, the firm may still be able to take you as a client.

Item 5B2: The preferred response here is zero. I would not eliminate a firm on this basis alone, but would want details about any history as a registered rep of a broker-dealer because this usually implies that the firm earns commissions on high-priced investment products sold to clients.

Item 5D: Most of the firm's clients should be individuals and "high-net worth" individuals (i.e., financial assets of $1 million or more).

Item 5E: Compensation Arrangements. Number 5 here is the red flag: as a general rule of thumb, you should never entrust your investments to a firm that derives any part of its income from commissions.

Item 5F(1) and (2): If the answer to (1) is No, this firm is not really an investment advisor or investment management firm it's probably a financial planning firm; that sells some insurance and/or investment products, and should be eliminated from consideration. In other words, the answer to (1) should be Yes, and (as noted above) the total US Dollar Amount of assets under management should be well in excess of $25 million.

Item 5G: Advisory Activities. If (2) is not checked, this firm is not really an investment management firm and should be eliminated from consideration.

Item 5I: Don't hire an advisor that sponsors or participates in wrap fee programs even if the firm has indicated that its compensation comes only from fees rather than commissions. For detailed discussion of wrap fee programs, see chapter 8, "The Financial Services Industry."

Item 6A: Other Business Activities. Preferably, none of these should be checked; ideally, you want the person managing your investments to be focused on that business to the exclusion of everything else. However, this is not a deal breaker.

Item 6B: The answer to this should be "No."

Item 8F: If the firm you are researching indicates that it compensates others for client referrals, you should ask them about such arrangements.

Item 9: Only at very large firms (e.g., Vanguard) is it okay for the firm itself to serve also as custodian of your assets. At smaller firms your assets should be held by a reputable third party custodian, NOT by the advisory firm itself. This is what ensures against a con artist decamping to Brazil with your savings or defrauding you in a Ponzi scheme.

Item 11: Disclosure Information. Every "No" box on this page should be checked because a "Yes" indicates that the firm has violated some of the laws and regulations governing registered investment advisors. Where a "Yes" has been checked, the firm must detail on the ADV the date and nature of the infraction, and how it was settled. A minor infraction, perhaps from some administrative error involving small amounts of money, may be forgiven, but any "Yes" on this page should be scrutinized closely and a firm that has multiple "Yes" boxes checked should *immediately* be tossed over the side of the boat.

On the page after Item 12, you'll find Part 2 of the ADV, which consists of the firm's own official brochure. This is not a marketing document, but one that conforms to a set structure and provides additional information on its investment philosophy, fee schedule, business practices, operations, code of ethics, and so on. Very instructive and should be read closely.

CHAPTER 2

How to Go It Alone

If you're not interested in investing or just don't have time do it right, this chapter is for you. Your plea is: just tell me what to do—and keep it simple and easy.

Okay. Bare minimum coming right up. But if you want reasons for these recommendations you're going to have to read the rest of the book.

First, as discussed in chapter 1, if you've already accumulated $50,000 or more outside of a 401(k) plan, you should consider shopping around for a good investment advisor to manage your money for you. Yes, you'll have to spend some time up front to make sure you select well, but then you can sit back and let someone else do the driving.

If you can't meet the minimum account size for independent advisors in your area, your simplest option is one of the online firms discussed in the previous chapter.

Anyway, before telling you what to do, I have to tell you what not to do.

DO NOT

• Walk into your nearest Merrill Lynch or Edward D. Jones or Morgan Stanley branch and say, "I need help." Avoid all such financial service firms. Their job is to make money for themselves and their shareholders, not for you.

• Invest with anyone who earns commissions on financial or investment products, or fees from wrap accounts. However capable, professional or charming they might be, their interests and yours are not properly aligned.

• Assume that a "financial planner" also has investment expertise. Chapter 1 explains how to differentiate those that do from those that don't.

• Invest in individual stocks or bonds. There's no reason whatsoever to believe you possess any stock- or bond-picking acumen.

• Invest mostly in actively managed mutual funds, whether load or no-load.

• Invest in hedge funds, hedge funds-of-funds, private equity, or private real estate partnerships.

• Just shove money into various randomly selected investment accounts. You must invest from the top down, allocating investments in a rational way that is designed to realize your objectives.

• Change the asset allocation of your investment portfolio because markets have gone up or down. You should only change your asset allocation if *your* circumstances change, not because market values fluctuate.

DO

• Write an investment policy statement that says who you are, what you are investing for, and how you intend to get there. By this I mean your total portfolio asset allocation and how this will be implemented across your various investment accounts, whether taxable or tax-deferred.

Two sample investment policy statements can be found in the appendix to this chapter.

If you skip this step, you'll be navigating without a map and will get lost.

• Commit to a regular, disciplined savings plan starting with maximum contributions to a 401(k) account if your employer offers one—especially if your company provides any matching contributions. If your company's 401(k) plan is not with a firm that offers low-cost index funds, you should try to persuade them to switch. A sample letter to this effect can be found in the Appendix at the end of this book. Your second savings priority should be to maximize contributions to an IRA account.

• Invest 401(k) and IRA money in low-cost index funds and/or exchange-traded funds (ETFs). Your best options are firms like Vanguard, Fidelity, and Schwab, which have the most choices at the lowest cost.

• Set up automatic monthly direct transfers from your bank account to fund a college savings plan and/or additional retirement savings at Fidelity, Vanguard, or Schwab.

• Rebalance the asset mix of your total investment portfolio back to the target allocations mapped out in your policy statement. This can be done by redirecting savings into whichever asset class[xiv] has gone down in value, or by selling some of what has gone up in value and using the proceeds to buy what has gone down. Rebalancing is absolutely counter-intuitive and absolutely necessary. Obviously you should consider the tax consequences of such moves and try to achieve as much as possible in tax-advantaged accounts. A good rebalancing rule of thumb recommended by author Larry Swedroe is to rebalance when an asset class has drifted from its target allocation by the lesser of 5 percentage points or 25%. Everyone knows they should diversify their investments; almost nobody realizes that if you don't rebalance you nullify the benefits of diversification.

HOW MUCH SHOULD YOU SAVE AND WHAT SHOULD YOU INVEST IN?

How Much Should You Save?

Schwab and Fidelity are among the companies providing excellent online tools you can use yourself to calculate how much you need to invest on a regular basis to reach a goal of x dollars in y years. They also help you figure out how much you'll need to have accumulated to enable you to withdraw x dollars each year for your retirement income.

What Should You Invest In?

Vanguard and Fidelity also offer tax-deferred 529 College Savings Plans that automatically select and subsequently adjust investment options based on the age of your child. These are called "Age-based portfolios" and provide an excellent way to save for college.[xv] Make sure you direct that the savings be invested in index funds, not actively managed options.

If you don't have a 401(k), a no-brainer alternative is Vanguard's Target Retirement Funds. With this choice, you don't have to make investment decisions at all; you just tell Vanguard what age you are and set up a regular transfer from your bank and Vanguard will allocate it for you.

If you're funding an IRA to the max, however, you might

want to hold bonds and REITs in your IRA since it's tax-deferred, while investing in stock index funds in taxable accounts. (REITS are real estate investment trusts; see the glossary for additional details.) If you do this, the most no-brainer equity fund to select is the Vanguard Total World Stock Index Fund. This is the closest you can get to a passive index fund that covers all the world's stock markets. Nothing could be simpler.

Why do I keep mentioning Vanguard, Schwab, and Fidelity? Because they offer a wide range of passive, low-cost index funds. And that's what you want. Actively managed index funds are more expensive and rarely add any value to compensate you for that expense. In fact, extensive research covering multiple time periods has shown that over the long haul you'll almost certainly suffer a double whammy from investing in actively managed stock or bond funds: higher costs and lower returns. And don't shrug that off: higher costs + lower returns might well = hundreds of thousands of dollars less for your retirement 25 or 30 years from now.

HOW TO ALLOCATE YOUR MONEY AMONG DIFFERENT INVESTMENTS

The financial services industry expends massive amounts of money and energy trying to sell you two falsehoods:

- First, that you should invest in whatever asset class or mutual fund has done well in recent years. This is dead wrong. Investment performance is *cyclical*, not linear; in other words, what has gone up will come down, and vice-versa. Investing in whatever has performed best in recent years is a sure-fire prescription for disappointing returns.

• Secondly, that what really matters is which investment manager (e.g., mutual fund) you select. No. The most important determinant of your portfolio's returns will be how it is allocated among various asset classes; in other words, how much to stocks, how much to bonds, and so on.

So how should you allocate your money? This is, was, and will be a topic of endless debate in the investment world (and is discussed more fully in chapter 12). However, since you're trying to keep things as simple as possible, you might just follow the allocation recommended in Vanguard's Target Retirement Funds program.

The key principle here is that younger savers should invest more in stocks than in bonds or cash, because stocks have a record of generating far higher returns than bonds or cash over periods of 20 years or longer. As one approaches the date when the money will be needed (e.g., for college tuition), the allocation to stocks should be cut back, because Murphy's Law dictates that the very year you need the money will be the year the stock market drops 50%.

The asset allocation for retirement savings is more complicated, because someone retiring at age 65, say, might reasonably hope to live another twenty years, and must plan for thirty years, because you don't want to run out of money before you run out of life. My advice to near retirees is to continue investing relatively heavily in US and foreign stock markets (e.g., up to 65% of assets), but to focus increasingly on index funds investing in larger, stable, dividend-paying companies rather than in the broad stock market or in funds focused on smaller companies.

CONCLUSION

That's it. If you resist the glittering allure of delusory promises dangled before you by the financial services industry and just follow these simple steps, you'll earn better returns than most investors and maximize the odds of realizing your financial goals:

1. Write a simple investment plan like those in the appendix to this chapter.
2. Allocate your savings to US and foreign stock market index funds, US Treasury and municipal bonds, and (in tax-deferred accounts) REITs and short-term corporate bonds.
3. The asset allocation should reflect your age and the purpose for which you are saving.
4. Invest in index funds whenever possible. Not just any index funds; make sure you select only low-cost index funds (or ETFs) offered by companies like Fidelity, Vanguard, and Schwab.

5. Rebalance among the different asset classes to ensure that you maintain the asset allocation laid out in
your investment plan. This means you have to sell
some of what has gone up in value and use the proceeds to buy more of what has gone down in value—
sometimes characterized as picking the flowers and
nurturing the weeds! Your guts will scream at you that
this is crazy, stupid, irrational, but it's not. The Ferris
wheel will turn; what is up will be down and what is
down will turn up. Just do it!

APPENDIX

The Investment Plan

The first two sample investment plans below are stripped down versions of those in chapter 12. The third (Jasmine Kimbara) is only given here.

Even if you are striving for minimalist simplicity, you must develop a written investment plan, or you'll almost certainly get sidetracked and lost along the way. As explained in chapter 12, I recommend that you write it in the third person. This will help you detach from the inevitable emotional roller coaster all investors experience and enable you stay on track.

Sample Investment Planning Document (I)

Peter Hardy's Investment Plan: January 1, 2013

Peter is 34 years old and single.

He is a quality-control manager at a pharmaceutical company.

His financial objective is to save 10% of his salary towards his retirement, over and above tax-deferred savings through maximum contributions to his firm's 401(k) plan and an IRA account.

1. The time horizon for the retirement fund is about 30 years.

2. Consequently, retirement savings should be invested 100% in stocks, now and for the next 20 years at least.

3. The volatility of global stock markets during this 30-year period is irrelevant and will generally be ignored.

4. The assets will be invested with an allocation of 30% in the Vanguard S&P 500 Index Fund, 20% in the Vanguard Extended Market Index Fund (US Small and Mid-Cap stocks), 30% in the Vanguard Developed Market Index Fund (Developed markets ex-US), and 20% in the Vanguard Emerging Markets Index Fund.

5. The investment account will grow by automatic monthly transfers from Peter's bank account to Vanguard.

6. Since differences in performance among the funds will result in the actual allocations shifting away from these target allocations, each year Peter will reset the allocation of these monthly transfers in order to bring the actual allocation back in line with the targets in #3.

7. He will stick with this plan through thick and thin, strenuously resisting all impulses to second-guess the economy and the markets. He will alter this plan only if his personal financial circumstances materially change in unforeseen ways.

Sample Investment Planning Document (II)

Tom and Sarah Minter's Investment Plan, January 1, 2013

Tom and Sarah Minter are both 58. Sarah plans to retire at the end of 2014 and Tom in five years.

Both their employers offer matching contributions to a 401(k) plan. For the past 15 years, Tom and Sarah have made the maximum possible contributions to both their 401(k) and their IRA accounts. In addition, they have managed to build up substantial additional savings in the past eight years.

A financial planner has advised them that from the date of Tom's retirement, they could reasonably expect their projected savings of $1,700,000 to generate $8,250 each month over 30 years, at which time they would run out of money. However, he has warned them that a sharp decline in portfolio value in the early years of retirement would result in a materially lower monthly income.

Tom and Sarah also intend to sell their house in Chicago and move to Florida when he retires, and they believe this move will increase their retirement savings, giving them a reasonable cushion against outliving their money.

1. The time horizon for the retirement fund is 30 years plus.

2. But starting in year six, the Minters plan to rely on this fund for most of their living expenses.

3. These expenses should be expected to rise at least in line with consumer price inflation. Consequently, the retirement fund should still be invested primarily in stocks, now and for the next 15 years at least, since bond returns are vulnerable to rising inflation.

4. However, stock market volatility could prevent the Minters from withdrawing enough money to sustain their standard of living. Consequently, they will invest 15% of their assets in intermediate Treasury bonds, 15% in high-quality municipal bonds, and 5% in Treasury Inflation Protected Securities (TIPS). These will help them sustain spending in the event of a severe bear market in equities early in Tom's retirement years.

5. The remaining 65% will be invested in stocks, with an emphasis on high-quality companies with a history of rising dividend payments.

6. The portfolio will be rebalanced annually to maintain this allocation.

7. The policy allocation of 65% to stocks, 15% to Treasury bonds, 15% to municipal bonds and 5% to TIPS will be implemented as follows: 50% in the Vanguard Dividend Growth Fund, 20% in the Vanguard Total International Stock Index Fund, 15% in the Vanguard Long-Term Tax-Exempt Fund, 15% in the Vanguard Intermediate-Term

Treasury Fund, and 5% in Vanguard's Inflation Protected Securities Fund.

8. Since differences in performance among the funds will shift the totals away from the target percentages, at the start of each year Tom and Sarah will rebalance their accounts back to the target allocations. This might require selling some funds that have done relatively well to invest in those that have done poorly, or deploying future savings into underweight funds until the target allocations are restored.

9. They will stick with this plan through thick and thin, strenuously resisting all impulses to second-guess the economy and the markets.

10. When Tom retires, the Minters will review their financial plan and this asset allocation policy to determine if it continues to meet their objectives.

Sample Investment Planning Document (III)

Jasmine Kimbara's Investment Plan, January 1, 2013

Jasmine is 25, single, and working as a financial analyst at a community bank, earning a modest salary. She rents a two-bedroom apartment, where she lives alone. She is trying to save enough to make a down payment on a small house, hopefully within five years, but she spends most of what she earns, except for small monthly contributions to her firm's 401(k) plan, which her employer matches up to 50%. Otherwise, she has no retirement fund and just enough savings to meet her expenses for three months, if for some reason she were to lose her job.

This is not really the kind of situation that calls for an investment plan. What Jasmine needs is a *financial* plan to help her realize her short-term goal of buying a house and encourage her to find ways to contribute a little more to her 401(k) and perhaps start an IRA account.

Of course, Jasmine's path in life is far more likely to change course than the Minters. She might get married and have children; at some point she'll probably change jobs; she might decide to go back to school, perhaps to earn an MBA or perhaps to switch careers entirely. Her priority right now is saving to buy a house rather than saving for retirement.

If she could do both, that would be great, but if not, her decision is that the house comes first. She's a financial analyst, so she should have no trouble working out how much she needs to save every month to reach the amount required for her down payment within five years. She should set up an automatic transfer from her bank account to Fidelity or Vanguard, to be deposited in a money market fund or low-cost short-term corporate bond fund. No stocks—her time horizon is too short—and no longer-term bond fund, because the value of such a fund could be hit by rising interest rates.

At current interest rates, she isn't going to earn much of

anything on this savings account, but she just has to accept that—any investment that offers a higher return also comes with greater risk, and Jasmine can't afford the risk of her savings losing value.

Part II

THE CAPITAL MARKETS

CHAPTER 3

The Capital Markets

INTRODUCTION

Whether going it alone or hiring an advisor, every investor should have at least some understanding of the capital markets. But most don't. In fact, even a rudimentary grasp of capital markets history gives you a competitive advantage because so many financial advisors and investment managers lack such knowledge.

Here's what you'll learn from this chapter:

- Long-term historical returns for stocks, bonds and cash

- The range of returns for stocks, bonds, and cash over different time periods

- The crucial difference between nominal (i.e., before inflation) and real (i.e., after inflation) returns

• The composition of stock returns

• Why stocks *should* generate higher returns than bonds or cash over longer time periods

• But how badly they can hurt you over shorter periods

• How stock market valuation indicators can tell you whether stock market returns are likely to fall at the high, middle or bottom end of their historical range over the next 10 or 15 years

• Why you should not invest in hedge funds, initial public offerings (IPOs), and private equity (venture capital and buyout funds)

• How the current yield of bonds is the best indicator of their likely future returns

• The different kinds of bonds and whether you should invest in them

WARNING!

As you've probably noticed, this book's a pretty easy read. And later chapters are a breeze too. But not this one. You're going to have to pay attention and digest reams of data, so I recommend a quiet spot and minimal distractions. And don't just zip through the tables and graphs in this section; if you study them closely and understand what they do and don't teach us, you'll lay the foundations for an intelligent approach to investing.

THE COMPOSITION OF INVESTMENT CAPITAL

There are two kinds of investment capital: equity and debt. Equity consists of full or partial ownership of a business or property, whether public (i.e., traded on the stock market) or private, while debt consists of money lent to a government, business, or person. If the maturity of that debt is 90 days or less, it is characterized as money-market investments.

According to McKinsey Global Institute, at year-end 2010 all the public debt and equity in the world amounted to $212 trillion. Of this, 25% was invested in stock markets and 75% in debt.

As of June 30, 2013, the Vanguard Total World Stock Index Fund, which is designed to mirror the FTSE Global All Cap Index of 7,400 stocks, was allocated as follows:

North America	52%
Europe	23%
Asia/Pacific	15%
Emerging Markets	10%

HISTORICAL CAPITAL MARKET RETURNS

Here are the nominal (i.e., before inflation) and real (i.e., after inflation) US$-based returns for global, US, and non-US stocks, bonds, and money market debt (bills) since 1900. [xvi]

AVERAGE ANNUAL HISTORICAL CAPITAL MARKET RETURNS						
Nominal Returns				**Real Returns**		
	Global	**US**	**Non-US**	**Global**	**US**	**Non-US**
Stocks	8.1%	9.4%	7.5%	5.0%	6.3%	4.4%
Bonds	4.8%	5.0%	4.4%	1.8%	2.0%	1.4%
Bills	3.9%	3.9%	3.9%	0.9%	0.9%	0.9%

As the data indicate, long-term investors have earned far more from stocks than from bonds or bills. In fact, by the end of 2012:

- $100 invested in the US stock market in 1900 would be worth $95,170 after inflation.

- $100 invested in the bond market would be worth only $940 after inflation.

- And $100 invested in the money markets only $270.

But the price of those higher stock market returns is much greater volatility and extended periods of pain:

- The worst single year for US stock market investors was 1931, with a return of -38%.

- But from its 1929 peak to the 1931 trough, the stock market declined 79% in real terms.

- 2008 wasn't far behind: in that year, US stocks returned -37.1% after inflation.

- And 2008 was the single worst year on record for global, non-US, and European stocks.

Those who recite the familiar mantra, "stocks for the long run" need to define just how long "the long run" needs to be. For US investors, the longest period of negative returns so far was the 16 years from 1905 to 1920, during which they earned -5% after inflation.

Elsewhere in the world, stock market investors have not always been so fortunate; for example, Japan, Germany and France have each experienced periods of 50 years or more during which their stock market generated negative cumulative real returns. In fact, most of the world's stock markets have suffered periods of at least two decades during which real cumulative returns were negative.

Bear markets can be brutal:

• During US bear markets, the S&P 500 has declined, on average, more than 40% from the previous bull market peak.

• And in doing so it has on average surrendered 83% of all the gains made during the preceding rise.

• In the most recent bear market of 2008-09, the S&P 500 declined 56.8% (second only to the 86.2% decline from September 1929 to June 1932), and surrendered just over 148% of the gains made from September 2001 to October 2007.

• Only those with sufficient time to recover from losses should invest in stocks.

Keep reading, and I'll explain just what I mean by "sufficient time" and why I believe US investors with time horizons extending beyond ten years should allocate most of their assets to stocks, regardless of their age.

THE RANGE OF REAL US STOCK MARKET RETURNS, 1900-1912

Here's a summary of the range of real US stock and bond returns over various rolling time periods since 1900 ("rolling" means 1900-49, 1901-50, 1902-51, etc.)

Periods	Average	High	Low	% Negative
Rolling 50-year periods (of which there are 757)				
Stocks	6.8%	9.5%	4.2%	0
Bonds	1.6%	3.5%	-0.7%	8.2%
Rolling 25-Year periods (of which there are 1057)				
Stocks	6.7%	12.6%	1.2%	0
Bonds	2.3%	8.3%	-2.6%	29.8%
Rolling 10-Year periods (of which there are 1237)				
Stocks	6.3%	20.1%	-5.9%	16.3%
Bonds	2.4%	12.5%	-5.8%	38.2%
Rolling 5-Year periods (of which there are 1297)				
Stocks	6.3%	33.8%	-13.7%	26.1%
Bonds	2.5%	19.8%	-12.4%	34.5%

Remember, I'm showing *real* returns here (i.e., after inflation), because if you earn a return of, say, 8% during a period when inflation has been running at 10%, it will *look* as if you have more money than when you started, but that's not much use if your money now buys less.

SUMMARY

- The *worst* five- and ten-year periods for US stocks and bonds have been about equally bad.

- But real bond returns have been negative far more often than have stock returns

- And while US stocks have always posted positive real returns over 25- and 50-year periods, bonds have not.

Exhibit 1
Distribution of Real Annual U.S. Stock Market Returns
1900–2012

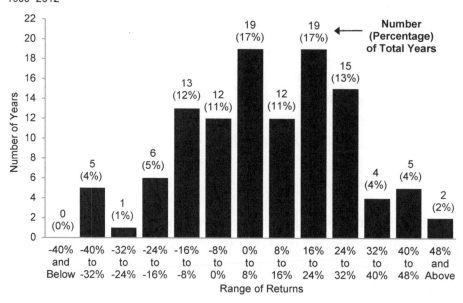

Note: Percentages may not total 100% due to rounding.

• Indeed, even over periods as long as 25 years, real returns on bond have been negative in almost *one-third* of all such periods.

• Such are the depredations of inflation and the reason, discussed in more detail below, why I believe US investors with time horizons extending beyond ten years should allocate no more than 35% of their assets to bonds, regardless of their age.

Exhibit 2
Distribution of Real Annual U.S. Bond Returns
1900–2012

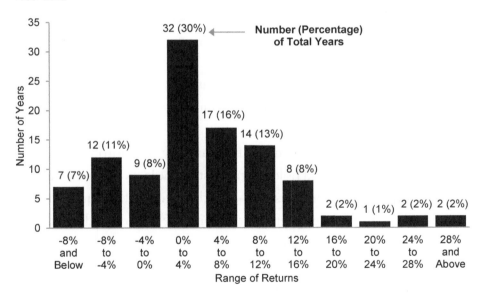

Note: Percentages may not total 100% due to rounding.

Making the Case for Stocks

However, this does not mean that stocks must necessarily outperform bonds in any given five-, 10- or even 20-year period. First, the only data we have is historical, and there is no guarantee that future returns will mirror those of the past. So it is entirely wrong and misleading to state that "US stocks outperform bonds in every period of 25 years or longer." Sure, US stocks *have* outperformed bonds in every period of 25 years or longer, but that verb tense change is critically important.

The case for stocks rests more on three premises than on the historical record.

• First, they are a claim on real assets rather than a claim on the nominal cash flows used to pay interest on debt.

• Second, they are far more volatile over short periods and therefore command a risk premium over bonds.

• Third, in the event that a company runs into financial difficulties, bond holders trump stock holders in their claim on the company's assets—in other words, the equity investors are at greater risk of losing their shirts and should get paid accordingly.

Although the historical record cannot tell us how events will unfold in the uncertain future, we should seek to learn from the history we have. So before looking in more detail at stocks and bonds separately, here are two additional exhibits summarizing the spread between stock and bond and stock and cash investments over one-, five-, 10- and 20-year periods from 1900 to 2012:

Exhibit 3
Excess Returns of U.S. Stocks Over Bonds
1900–2012 • Rolling Monthly Periods

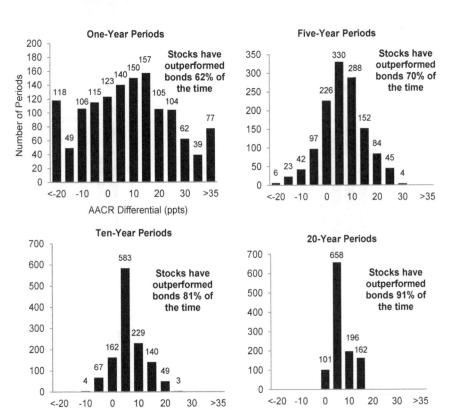

Note: AACR represents the average annual compound return.

Exhibit 4
Excess Returns of U.S. Stocks Over Cash
1900–2012 • Rolling Monthly Periods

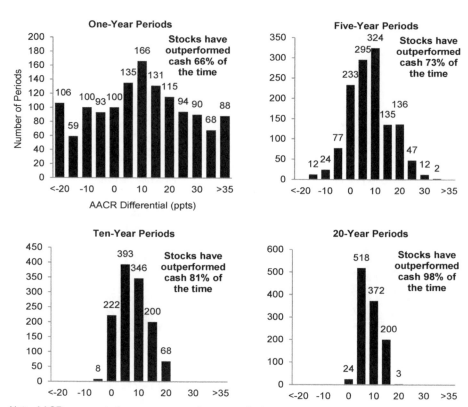

Note: AACR represents the average annual compound return.

Summary of Capital Markets History

• All our data on capital market returns are historical and we should not assume that the future pattern of returns will mirror that of the past.

• Nevertheless, capitalism only works if those incurring the greater risk of investing in stocks have some reasonable prospect of earning higher returns than those incurring the lesser risk of investing in bonds, especially over the long term.

• Since 1900, stocks have outperformed bonds, on average, by about 4.0 percentage points or better in one-, five-, 10- and 20-year periods and have outperformed money market investments, on average by 5.5 percentage points or better over these same periods. Compounded over time, this has resulted in a huge difference in cumulative wealth in favor of stock market investors.

• But beware of averages! The width of the distribution around the average is as important as the average itself. The wider the range, the less chance you have of actually earning the average. There have been some periods of as long as 20 years in which US bonds have outperformed US stocks. However, even over periods as short as five years, stocks have outperformed bonds more often than not.

• Historically, the worst five- and 10-year periods for stocks and bonds have been equally bad, but the real return of bonds has been negative far more often.

A SHORT PRIMER ON EQUITIES

Investing in Public Equities (Stocks)

The returns on an investment in the stock of a public company come from three sources: the current dividend, the real growth of that dividend, and changes in valuation. Jack Bogle sensibly characterizes the first two as "fundamental" sources of return and the third as "speculative."[xvii]

The starting dividend yield + real dividend growth has accounted for almost 90% of the stock market's long-term return, with the remaining 10% attributable to the fact that the dividend yield of the stock market has declined from over 5% a hundred years ago, to 2.1% today.

Reinvestment of dividends is responsible for almost 40% of investors' total return on US stocks since 1900.

• If you had invested $100 in the US stock market in 1900 and spent your dividends along the way, your portfolio would be worth $758 at the end of 2012, after adjusting for inflation.

• That's an average annual real return of 1.8%.

• On the other hand, if you had reinvested all those dividends, you'd now have $80,277 after inflation (assuming this was in a tax-free account).

• The result: an average annual real return of 6.1%

What about earnings? Earnings are what we hear about on CNBC. Earnings are what analysts pore over. Stock reports discuss what guidance management has given about next quarter's earnings and when a company announces its earnings, its stock often rises or falls depending on whether it "beat" consensus earnings estimates or fell short. So isn't it all about earnings?

Not really. It should be more about dividends.

Think about it: how do you hope to make money owning a company's stock? What might cause it to rise or fall in price? You assume that if the company's earnings increase, the stock price will reflect this by appreciating. But why? How do investors benefit from higher earnings? If investor A pays $22 for a share of Intel, why might investor B buy it from him for $30 two years later? Intel doesn't pay out its earnings to its investors; it pays out some of its earnings in the form of a dividend. The stock appreciates in price only if Intel keeps raising that dividend so that its shareholders share in the benefits of its increased earnings--or if investors expect that Intel will be bought out.

So although rising earnings are important, they are not an end in themselves. They allow companies to finance growth and keep distributing cash to their shareholders. This is true even of companies that currently pay no dividend because they are reinvesting all their profits back into the business to fuel additional growth. At the end of the day, even

Google or Facebook or any other company is only worth whatever profits it can distribute to its shareholders.

That's the whole point of any business, large or small—to generate profits that can be distributed to the owners or make the company's selling price higher one day.

Why, then, do we read and hear so much about earnings and so little about dividends? Because dividends don't benefit Wall Street. As many commentators have remarked, the whole quarterly earnings circus is an elaborate farce. Companies routinely massage earnings to ensure that they can report a number slightly better than consensus estimates; armies of analysts pump out reams of reports picking these numbers apart; stocks are rated "buy," "hold," or "sell" on the basis of all this data-crunching. What's it all about?

For Wall Street, it's all about transactions: sell this, buy that—do something, don't just sit there and collect or reinvest your dividends. When a well-managed company sticks to its knitting, runs its business well and steadily raises its dividend payment to shareholders, who gets paid? Shareholders, of course, but not the brokers and investment bankers—that sane approach is no good for them. The investment bankers make money by persuading companies to use excess profits for mergers and acquisitions, rather than cash payments to shareholders. And the brokers make money persuading you to sell Boeing and buy IBM, or vice-versa, on the basis of their analysts' recommendations.

As Daniel Peris points out in *The Strategic Dividend Investor*, if one slices the US stock market into quartiles based on dividend yield, the best performing stocks have been those with the highest dividend yield, not those with the fastest growth. The highest-yielding quartile has also been the least volatile. That's more return with less risk—a rare combination. In a particularly telling example, he notes that from the first year of NASDAQ stock data, 1971, through mid-2010, the excruciatingly boring utility sector, as represented by the S&P Utilities Index, outperformed the NASDAQ Index (consisting largely of smaller growth companies) by 50 basis points a year (i.e., ½% annually).[xviii]

Summary of Investing in Public Equities

The purpose of any capitalist enterprise is to make money. In the case of companies that raise capital by selling stock to investors, the only reason for investors to provide this capital is the expectation that they will receive some of the company's profits or make money selling the business.

If you sink money into a stock in the vague hope that someday, someone somewhere will buy it from you at a higher price, but you really have no idea why this might come about, you are engaged in speculation, not investing.

Shareholders would be better served if companies headlined current and prospective dividend payments in their quarterly reports, rather than earnings. Earnings are an accounting construct that can be readily massaged; dividend payments are hard cash.

But don't hold your breath: most of the capital companies need flows through Wall Street, and any such move would antagonize the bankers and brokers whose living depends on transactions.

Stock Market Valuation

Historically, investors have focused on three valuation metrics that can be applied both to individual stocks and to the stock market as a whole. These are:

1) **The price: book ratio (P/B),** the current price of the stock or stock market (e.g., the S&P 500 index) divided by its book value or the book value of all the companies in the S&P 500. Book value is computed by dividing the value of a company's equity by the number of shares outstanding. Thus, if Company A's equity value is $10 billion and it has 5 billion shares outstanding, its book value is 2.

- Since 1929, the P/B ratio for the companies comprising the S&P Industrials index has averaged 2.1.

- The lowest point was 0.4 on June 30, 1932.

- The highest point was 6.0 on December 31, 1999.

- The current P/B ratio is about 2.4.

As the composition of the US economy has shifted increasingly from manufacturing to services,[xix] this valuation metric has become less useful, since the book value of service companies is not very relevant to their enterprise value.

2) **The dividend yield.** If Company A's stock price is $25 and it pays a dividend of $1 per year, then its dividend yield is 4% (1÷25).

- For the 113 years from 1900 to 2012, the average dividend yield of the S&P 500 was 4.3%.

- But the dividend yield in the first half of the twentieth century was far higher, at 5.4%, than it has been subsequently, at 3.2%.

- And since the mid-1980s the trend has been towards even lower dividend payouts.

- As of June 30, 2013, the S&P 500's dividend yield was 2.1% and that of Non-US stock markets was 2.6%.

3) **The price: earnings ratio (P/E).** This is the current price of the stock or stock market (e.g., S&P 500) divided by the earnings per share of the stock or of all the companies comprising that index.

• There are several versions of the P/E, depending on whether the calculation is based on operating or reported earnings, trailing 12-month or prospective 12-month earnings, and so on.

• By far the best measure is the cyclically-adjusted P/E, or CAPE, also known as the Shiller P/E after Robert Shiller of Yale University.

• Because year-to-year earnings are quite volatile, this measure averages earnings out over 10 years, making the "E" in the P/E ratio more stable

• This is my favorite stock market valuation metric; much analysis shows that it is most predictive of future returns. We'll come back to this in detail below.

The Composition of Stock Market Returns

Changes in valuation can have a profound effect on returns. For example, let's assume that the earnings of the S&P 500 grow by 4.4% over the next five years--the average annual growth rate of US corporate earnings since 1960. And that the P/E of the S&P 500 index is 20 and its price is 1200. But at the end of that five years, when you're ready to sell, the P/E has declined to 10. Despite perfectly respectable earnings growth, the index will now be priced at 744—ouch!

But as Charley Ellis wisely advises, we should try to ignore the short-term antics of Mr. Market and concentrate on long-term fundamentals. So what has been the fundamental return to stock investors?

To answer this question, Cambridge Associates has looked at every period lasting at least 40 years, from 1900-to date, when the stock market's P/E at the beginning and end of the period was just about the same.

• For example, the P/E in 1901 was 14.3 and in 1987 it was 14.1. The average dividend yield over those 87 years was 4.8% and the real compound earnings growth rate was 1.0. On this basis, one would assume that the total average annual real compound return for this period would be 5.8% (4.8 + 1). And indeed it was exactly that.

• Not all such periods match up so precisely, but the disparities are relatively small. For example, in 1935 the stock market's P/E was 19.4 and at the end of 1996 it was 19.1. Close enough.

• Average dividend yield over those 62 years was 4.2% and real compound earnings growth, 3.1%. The estimated return would therefore be 7.3% (4.2 + 3.1), but the actual return for this period was 7.6%.

• For the 19 periods meeting the eligibility criteria, that average beginning and ending P/E was 13.7, the average estimated return (based on average dividend yield + real earnings growth) was 6.4% and the average actual return, 6.5%.

In short, although changes in valuation can certainly affect returns for any given period—and sometimes quite dramatically—over the long-term, it is dividends and real dividend (or earnings) growth that ultimately generates returns.

Can reading valuation tea leaves ever help us invest more effectively?

Historical Stock Market Valuations

Price-Earnings Ratio

We all know the familiar mantra: buy low, sell high. But how can we recognize "low" and "high"? As noted above, one of the best ways to gauge the stock market's value is the cyclically-adjusted price-earnings ratio (CAPE), which is computed by dividing the current price of the S&P 500 index by the annualized average real earnings-per-share of the S&P 500 constituent companies over the past ten years.

The historical average for this ratio since 1970 is 16.0. As of June 30, 2013, it was just over 23.0, meaning that the stock market was somewhat overvalued at that time.[xx] But it has ranged from as much as 45 to as low as 7, as I'll discuss below.

What we can learn from this history is that investors are manic-depressive. Or to put it more conventionally, they are subject to irrational outbursts of greed and fear.

Exhibit 5
S&P 500 Cyclically Adjusted P/E Ratios
1910–2013

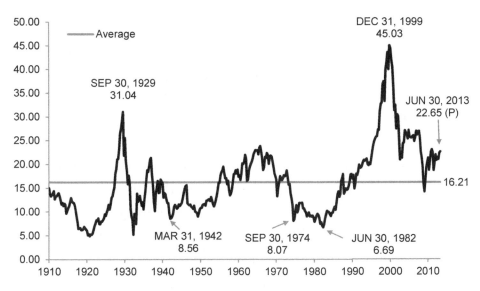

Notes: (P) Preliminary. Normalized real price-earnings ratios for the S&P 500 Index are calculated by dividing the current index value by the annualized average real earnings for the trailing ten years. Graph represents quarterly data.

What does CAPE actually mean and what can we learn from it?

• Investors have been prepared to pay as much as $45 for every $1 of stock market earnings at some times, and at others they won't go much higher than $7.

• Collectively, they are anticipating whether future earnings will be higher or lower than today's. Since earnings rise and fall quite dramatically in economic expansions and contractions, there's a lot of guesswork involved.

• For example, since 1900 the real earnings per share of the S&P 500 companies has declined, on average, by 41.3% during recessions. The worst-ever decline was the most recent: from June 30, 2007 to March 32, 2009, S&P 500 earnings dropped by a stunning 92.1%.[xxi]

• It would be rational for investors to assume that if earnings have been particularly strong, they'll revert to their long-term average, and if they've been crushed by recession they'll recover. But investors aren't rational. Look at the almost vertical ascent of the CAPE to the peak in 1929 at the end of the madcap 1920s, and again, even more dramatically, to the loony-toons level of 45.0 at the end of 1999. That's when the Fed flooded the economy with excess dollars to offset a possible "Y2K" computer fiasco at the turn of the millennium, which had about the same effect as pouring gasoline on a raging fire. Do you remember how sure everyone was that the dot.com era had ushered in a new age? That although stock prices were certainly high, they could only go higher because everything was different this time around? Right.

• What history tells us is that investor sentiment gets in the way of rational decision-making: as the economy rolls over into recession and stock prices drop in anticipation of worse times ahead, investor sentiment shifts from optimism to pessimism; and as the economy starts booming, from pessimism to optimism.

• By mid-1982, stock market investors had suffered a long battering, with average annual real returns of -3.9% over the preceding 10 years, while the economy was mired in stagflation and interest rates at unprecedented highs. That CAPE of 6.7 in June 1982 reflects the deep gloom of investors unable to perceive that the most powerful bull market in the history of US capitalism was about to take off.

• By the end of 1999, of course, this incredible boom had led investors to the opposite extreme, where they were paying the ludicrous price of $45 for every $1 of S&P 500 earnings—a CAPE that implied a rate of future earnings growth totally off the charts.

• In short, extreme CAPE readings—although relatively rare—can be very instructive for long-term investors. If we take all the quarterly S&P 500 CAPE ratios since 1910, and divide them into quartiles, from low to high, and then look at subsequent 15-year real average annual compound returns, this is what we find:

CAPE Ratio Quartiles		Subsequent 15-Year Real AACR
First	8.2	10.3%
Second	11.6	9.6%
Third	15.3	6.2%
Fourth	20.5	2.7%

The basic message is unambiguous: when the CAPE has been low, subsequent returns have been high; when the CAPE has been high, subsequent returns have been low.

"The dilemma facing investors," writes John Ameriks of Vanguard, "is that they do not know whether they will be investing over a 'best,' 'worst," or 'average' period." That's almost certainly true—and the shorter the period the truer it is. But as the table above shows, for longer periods we can in fact arrive at a well-educated guesstimate, based on current valuations.

So long-term investors should keep an occasional eye on the CAPE. Most of the time, it won't tell you much and you should not tinker with your portfolio on the basis of short-term swings in this ratio. But when it soars way above or plunges deeply below its long-term average range, you should pay attention, since it serves as a useful reminder that when the stock market goes way up, sooner or later it will come way back down, and vice-versa.

DIVIDEND YIELD

Since the three components of return are dividend yield, real dividend or earnings growth, and changes in valuation, dividends matter. As John Burr Williams wrote in *The Theory of Investment Value* back in 1938:

> *A cow for her milk,*
> *A hen for her eggs,*

And a stock, by heck,
For her dividends.[xxii]

Because dividends are such an essential component of re-turns, the stock market's current dividend yield plays an important role in market valuation analysis. Or should. Instead, during the great bull market of 1982-99, the fuddy-duddy notion that one bought stocks for their dividends fell into a coma, from which it is only now beginning to recover as investors have re-discovered that stock prices can fall as well as rise.

Although the S&P 500's long-term average dividend yield is 4.3%, it fell as low as 1.1% in 1999 and has averaged only 2.1% over the past 20 years. Why? Many companies decided that using surplus cash to buy back shares was a more shareholder-friendly use of funds than paying out more in dividends, largely because of taxes. At one point, the long-term capital gains investors would realize that the shares they sold were subject to lower tax rates than dividends. But in 2003 this argument was rendered moot when taxes on both long-term capital gains and dividends were reduced to 15%.

Historically, low dividend yields have served as an indicator of market over-valuation, and high dividend yields as an indicator of market under-valuation. Now the longish decline in dividend yields confuses the picture and it's impossible to determine whether the trend will continue or reverse.

The sum of current dividend yield and subsequent real growth of dividend distributions will determine the stock market's future return (net of changes in the price-earnings multiple). Investors ignore those numbers at their peril. So let's do the elementary math required:

• The invaluable data on Robert Shiller's website shows that since 1926 the real dividend growth rate of the S&P 500 has averaged 2.3%.

• The S&P 500 currently pays a dividend yield of 2.1%.

• For the market to match its long-term average annual real return of 6.1% (1900-2012) over, say, the next five years, dividends must therefore grow at a rate of 4.2%, after inflation—assuming the P/E is the same at the end of that period as it is today.

• Corporate America is currently flush with cash—well over $1.5 trillion—and so it's possible companies might be disposed to raise dividends more aggressively as a result of shareholder prodding. Nevertheless, since the *nominal* growth rate of dividends over the long term has been 4.4%, a 4.2% *real* dividend growth rate is a pretty tall order.

Venture Capital and Buyout Investing

Not all equity is publicly traded—far from it—and so I'll conclude this review of equity investing with some warnings about the lure of private equity investing.

For as long as recorded history people have invested goods and money in trading enterprises, hoping to increase their stock of material wealth. In other words, venture capital investing existed centuries before that term was coined. I can't advise you on whether you should pour your savings into that business you've always dreamed of starting, nor on whether you should back your visionary brother-in-law, except to note that most new businesses fail.

The world is full of people with terrific ideas and the United States in particular has a great history and culture of encouraging innovators to launch new businesses, and of not stigmatizing those who fail. Investors go wrong, however, when they focus too much on the business idea. What really determines the outcome is the business capability of the entrepreneur. Good entrepreneurs are scarce.

Businesses fail primarily because the founders' expectations are too optimistic, they have no fallback plan for when things (inevitably) go wrong, and they are inadequately capitalized at the outset.[xxiii]

So if you're ever approached by a friend or associate looking to raise money to launch a great new product, the key question isn't, "Is this a viable product?" but "Does this person have any sort of track record of starting successful businesses from scratch?" I use the plural deliberately. I'm a great admirer of successful entrepreneurs, but wary of assuming that because someone has succeeded in founding, managing, and selling a new business, he or she can necessarily repeat that success. So much depends on fortuitous timing and other forms of good luck that I'd be reluctant to open my wallet for a one-timer launching his second venture.

However, I can definitely advise you on whether to invest in professionally managed venture capital funds (which then deploy their investors' capital into new enterprises). Don't. Unless you have assets upwards of $100 million and can afford to hire Cambridge Associates to advise you, the chances of your realizing decent returns from any venture capital fund you've been recommended are slim to none. Venture capital returns are intensely concentrated in a few mega-hits, like E-Bay or Google, whose early-stage funding has come from venture capital firms you can't access because they are either closed to new investors or inaccessible to individuals like you and me.

Research has shown that even most institutional investors--pension funds, corporations, and insurance companies, and others--would have earned better returns investing in public equity markets than in the venture capital funds they selected. In fact, as a group, the only successful venture investors are major endowments and foundations, and some very wealthy individuals or family offices who have access to leading venture funds through personal connections or professional expertise.

So if you are offered an "opportunity" to invest in such-and-such a venture capital fund—or fund-of-funds—don't bite. I'm afraid it's as simple as this: if they want your money, you don't want them. The sellers have strong incentives to reel you in because they earn large commissions on the money they raise; and the fund managers have strong incentives to gather assets because they charge very high fees. All in all, it's a swell deal for everyone except the hapless investors. The history tells it all: big promises followed by lousy returns.

The same goes for buyout funds, whose objective is to buy weak or poorly-managed companies (public or private), improve their performance and then sell them at a large profit, either by listing them on the stock market or by selling to another company. Again, only a few buyout specialists have consistently generated good returns for their investors, net of all fees and expenses, and they don't want or need your money. So my advice is the same: stay away. Over time, you will almost certainly do better investing in the stock market.

INITIAL PUBLIC OFFERINGS (IPOS)

Venture capital and buyout firms realize the return on their investments in one of two ways: either they sell the companies they've invested in to other buyers, whether public or private, or they list them on a stock exchange through initial public offerings, or IPOs—in other words, sell stock to investors.

So if you get a chance to invest in an IPO, should you bite? Could be the next Google, right? Or not. Actually, almost certainly not. After all, Google was only one of over 9,500 IPOs listed since 1975. If you check out the track record of all these new issues at http://bear.cba.ufl.edu/ritter/ipodata.htm, which is maintained by University of Florida finance prof Jay Ritter, you'll be shocked by how badly they've performed, compared to the US stock market in general.[xxiv]

Hedge Funds

There are now approximately 9,000 hedge funds with about $2.1 trillion in assets under management. However, the attrition rate is ferocious—citing an article in the publication *Pensions & Investments*, Goldie and Murray report that "fewer than 15 percent of hedge funds last longer than six years, and 60 percent of them disappear in less than three years."[xxv]

Because they typically charge 1.5% or 2.0% in fees on assets under management plus 20% of profits, hedge fund managers must leap over a very high bar to generate net returns to investors better than those investors could earn in a portfolio of stock and bond index funds. All the available research shows that very few succeed in doing so and that none of the top hedge funds are accessible to retail investors. This applies equally to those that are long/short equity investors (which is about half of all hedge funds) and to those engaged in more esoteric practices like market neutral, pairs trading, event arbitrage, and distressed investing.[xxvi] Don't believe any brokers or advisors who tell you their firm's hedge fund-of-funds has access to the best managers. The tiny percentage of hedge funds (perhaps 2% of the industry total) that have in fact generated decent returns, net of fees, and might have a reasonable chance of doing so in the future, generally shun funds-of-funds like the plague. If they are accepting new capital (and many are not), it's only from qualified institutional investors.

Both hedge funds and funds-of-funds have in fact generated spectacular returns—for themselves, but not their investors. In his devastating critique of the industry, insider Simon Lack estimates that since the 1990s, 98% of all the returns generated by hedge funds have been consumed by manager fees. That's $440 billion to the managers, leaving $9 billion to their investors—almost all of whom would have realized far higher returns investing in an index-fund portfolio of 60% stocks/40% bonds.[xxvii]

The bottom line is simple: from your perspective, hedge funds are simply an effective mechanism for transferring wealth from chumps to investment managers. Stay away!

Summary of Equity Investing

Even over long periods, stock market returns deviate significantly from their long-term average. And the primary determinant of returns for any given period is starting valuations. If you invest when valuations are extremely high, your subsequent returns will be relatively low, and vice-versa.

The cliché that investors swing from greed to fear and back again is bang on target. Stock market returns have always reverted from high to low and low to high again, cycling around their long-term mean return of about 6% after in-flation.

So young investors should rejoice if they are starting to save when markets have been battered; they're buying cheap. Investors approaching retirement should keep a weather-eye on valuations and trim their exposure to stocks if the cyclically-adjusted price-earnings ratio soars into extreme territory—because this signifies storms ahead when investor optimism turns to fear, and the worst possible time to start withdrawing money from your nest egg is when markets have crashed.

As chapter 13 discusses, thinking clearly requires overriding our instincts. This is the first and most important step in managing risk.

A SHORT PRIMER ON BONDS

Bond Math 101

How bond prices move in the opposite direction of interest rates.

• If Jane invests $10,000 in a Treasury bond that pays 5%, she'll receive $500 a year in two semi-annual payments of $250.

• If interest rates rise over the next two years, so that new issues are now paying 6%, she should cash in her old bond and use the $10,000 to buy a new one that will pay her $600 a year, yes? Alas, no!

• *Because* interest rates have risen, Jane's old bond won't sell for $10,000; she'll only get $8,333. How so?

• Because if Joe buys Jane's bond for that amount, the $500 it pays in annual interest will amount to 6% of his purchase price. In other words, Jane's bond will decline in price to whatever level results in its yielding the same as new bonds.

• On the other hand, if interest rates on new bonds drop from 5% to 4%, then Jane's bond will be worth $12,500, since that's the price at which her $500 a year payments equal 4% of the purchase price.

• Of course, there's no point in Jane's selling her bond at that price, unless she wants to spend the money, because that's what it would cost her to buy another bond yielding $500 a year. Plus she'd incur transaction costs that would nibble away at her capital.

In short, a Treasury bond's price moves in the opposite direction of interest rates. So if rates go up, bond prices go down, and vice-versa.

However, this math only applies to Treasury bonds, because they are backed by "the full faith and credit" of the United States government, and the highest quality corporate bonds.

In a recession, interest rates typically *decline* because the demand for credit dries up. Treasury-bond prices generally rise more than those of other bonds because investors become more risk averse and rush to buy this safest of assets. However, weaker credits (i.e., lower-quality corporate bonds) typically decline in price during a recession because investors demand higher yields to compensate for the increased possibility that the companies issuing the bonds might run into financial trouble and default.[xxviii]

Corporate Debt

A public company raises capital by selling equity (i.e., shares of stock) and debt (i.e., bonds). Part of the chief financial officer's job is figuring out the optimum mix of the two, given the company's financing needs and the cost to the company at that time.

Most corporate bond issues have a "call" feature that allows the issuer to buy back the bonds at a pre-determined price at set dates before the bond matures. Companies benefit when they sell bonds at the lowest possible interest rate, and if interest rates subsequently decline, call in older bonds issued at higher rates and sell new ones in their stead. Senior management usually enjoy stock option plans, which—if properly structured—align their interests with those of the shareholders. They have a stake in the value of the company's shares. But they don't own or have any interest in the company's debt, and so may manage the company in such a way as to benefit shareholders at the expense of bondholders.

In defense, bonds typically include rules that prevent re-calls before a certain date and require the company to meet criteria that ensure its ability keep paying interest. Failure to meet these conditions means bondholders can gain control of the company, wiping out shareholders' equity and, if nec-essary, liquidating the company's assets to get at least some of their money back.

So the virtue of bonds is that they are higher up the food chain: as long as a company has sufficient cash flow, it must pay interest on its debt before paying shareholders any divi-dends, and if the company fails, bondholders salvage what they can from the carcass, and shareholders get nothing.

For these reasons, bonds are less risky than stocks:

• Since 1900, the worst three-year annualized return for US corporate bonds is -6.9%; for US stocks it is -42.7%.

• Similarly, the worst five-year annualized return for bonds is -2.9%; for stocks -18.0%.

• There is no 10-year period during which bonds have posted a negative return; in their worst decade, bonds posted a slight positive return of 0.4%. Stocks returned -5.4% in their worst decade.

But bonds suffer from two serious defects. First, they have an asymmetric risk:return profile: the upside is limited and the downside potential is large. The expected return on a bond is the yield-to-maturity, which is about the same as what it currently pays, expressed as a percentage of the current price. It can't go higher; it's limited.

However, if a company falls on hard times, even bond-holders may end up with little more than pennies on the dollar.

This risk can be reduced by owning a diversified mix of bonds, but it's still there.

The other problem is inflation. Most bonds pay interest in nominal dollars and so the real value of those payments shrinks with inflation. In other words, the price of stability is a lack of growth.

Going back to our comparison of stock and bond returns since 1900, we find that if we look at real returns (i.e., returns after inflation), bonds don't look so hot:

- The worst three-year real annualized return for US corporate bonds was -16.8%; for US stocks, -38.1%.

- The worst five-year period was -12.4%, vs. -13.7% for stocks.

- In their worst 10-year period the real return on bonds was -5.8%, vs. -5.9% for stocks.

- If we keep going, bonds have been the loser: the worst 20-year real cumulative return for bonds was -3.3% compared to -0.6% for stocks, and over 25 years, -2.6% for bonds and +1.2% for stocks.

Types of Bonds

For simplicity's sake, I've used conventional corporate bonds as representative of bonds in general, but in fact about two-thirds of the world's bonds are issued by governments rather than corporations.

US investors can think of bonds as belonging to any of five camps:

1. Treasury and agency bonds issued by the US government.

2. Treasury Inflation Protected Securities (TIPS), also issued by the US Treasury.

3. Corporate bonds issued by public companies.

4. Tax-free municipal bonds issued by state and local governments.

5. Foreign bonds, both sovereign and corporate.

TREASURIES

Despite rumblings from financially illiterate ideologues who believe it might be quite salutary for the US government to default on its debt obligations, Uncle Sam's bills, notes, and bonds[xxix] are still regarded as free of any credit risk.

TREASURY INFLATION PROTECTED SECURITIES (TIPS)

What about inflation-linked bonds? Some experts believe these should comprise a significant percentage of individuals' retirement savings since they combine the superior stability of Treasury bonds with inflation protection.

I don't agree.

The United States first issued Treasury Inflation Protected Securities (TIPS) in 1997, and so the record is relatively short. However, UK inflation-linked bonds date back to 1981, giving us 30 years of history to ponder. Surprisingly, the first thing that stands out is that these linkers (as they are called in the UK) have shown no correlation with UK inflation (experts differ over why this has been so).

Secondly, the return to investors has been miserable (which means, in effect, that the government has prospered at investors' expense). When US TIPS were first issued, they offered a real yield of 4%, which was a terrific bargain; the average annual real return on US corporate bonds has been 2.4% since 1900. However, real yields have been far lower in recent years, only 0.20% for 10-year TIPS, up from a recent low of -0.75%.

- Historically, the real yields on TIPS have tracked the nominal yields of conventional government bonds. So if interest rates rise in future years—as seems inevitable given how low they are today—then the price of TIPS will decline, as will those of conventional Treasury bonds and notes.

• This decline may be offset to a greater or lesser extent by TIPS' inflation adjustment. For example, if we assume inflation rises over the next five years, as the Federal Reserve's efforts to stimulate the economy gain some traction, then the value of a TIP will adjust upwards with rising inflation.

• So rising inflation will boost the price of TIPS, while rising interest rates will shove prices down.

• The bottom line is that TIPS will provide *some* inflation protection, but probably not as much as their advocates assume.

• If my purpose is to ensure that I have an asset that will appreciate at least in line with rising inflation, this is only guaranteed to work if I bought the TIP when issued and hold it until it matures.

• Of course, if you extend the time horizon, holding TIPS for 10 or 20 years, then the odds of keeping pace with inflation improve, but so do the odds of stocks generating far higher real returns.

There are two kinds of inflationary periods that are bad for stocks: when inflation rises far faster than expected and when high inflation coincides with economic stagnation (stagflation).

Because they are free of credit risk *and* tied to inflation, TIPS are an ideal hedge against stagflation; their returns will be boosted both by the high inflation and by investors' propensity to favor government bonds during periods of economic stress.

As explained above, TIPS may not perform as well during an inflationary spike if their rise in price from rising inflation is offset to some extent by rising real yields, which would push their price in the opposite direction.

In short, it's a good idea to allocate a small percentage of your assets to TIPS (in tax-deferred accounts) as a hedge against stagflation. However, larger allocations to TIPS should be considered only when they offer real yields of about 2.5% or better.

CORPORATE BONDS

Not so for corporate bonds whose credit quality is rated by agencies like Moody's and Standard & Poor's. These bonds are characterized as "investment grade" if they are rated BBB- or better, on a scale of AAA (immaculate creditworthiness) to D (in default).[xxx] The lower the bond rating of a company, the higher the interest rate it must pay to attract investors since a lower rating implies a higher risk of default.

TAX-EXEMPT MUNICIPAL BONDS (MUNIS)

These are also rated by the rating agencies, using the same credit-rating system as that for corporate bonds.

When the financial crisis and subsequent recession of 2008-09 smashed state and local government revenues, throwing them into deep deficits, many commentators raised the specter of widespread muni-bond defaults, most notably Meredith Whitney on a 60 *Minutes* show in late 2010. Ms. Whitney predicted an Armageddon of "hundreds of billions of dollars" in defaults as the fiscal crisis deepened.

In the $3 trillion muni-bond market this would amount to a default rate of 7%, compared to an average annual default rate of 0.01% over the past 40 years, and a peak default rate of 0.4% in 1991. In fact, since 1980, only 47 US municipalities (i.e., cities, town, counties) have filed for bankruptcy. By way of comparison, 14,000 US corporations filed for bankruptcy in 2010 alone.

For sure, many state and local governments have had a tough row to hoe and a steep hill ahead, but except for some lower-quality, speculative issues, there won't be widespread defaults—certainly not to the tune of "hundreds of billions of dollars," or anything close to that number.

For taxpayers in the maximum federal tax bracket (now 39.6%), the taxable equivalent yield of long-maturity muni-bonds has averaged 185% of the yield on long-maturity Treasuries. As of June 30, 2013, however, the taxable equivalent yield was 2.07%. Although this suggests that munis are relatively attractive to such investors, it's worth noting that both Treasury and muni-bond yields have recently plumbed historical lows from which they are almost certain to rise in the years ahead.

As bond yields rise, bond prices decline. So bondholders intending to sell their bonds (or bond funds) in the next few years should consider whether it might be better to sell sooner rather than later. But if your bond fund is a long-term holding, with dividends reinvested, the reinvestment of higher yields over the years will eventually offset any decline in price. In other words, if your time horizon is short, you should be worried about rising interest rates; if your time horizon is long, you shouldn't.

NON-US BONDS

There's no compelling reason for individual investors to own foreign bonds or bond funds. They're more expensive to buy and own than their domestic counterparts and they come with greater risk but no higher return. In addition, they don't necessarily provide US investors with the same protection against financial or economic crises that US Treasury bonds provide. Hence they're a lose-lose proposition.

Your friendly local broker may try to tempt you into a foreign bond fund with promises of higher yields than those of domestic bond funds, but this is illusory. When two countries have different rates of inflation, the one with the higher rate has to pay higher nominal interest on its bonds to compensate investors. Thus, the real rate of return will prove the same, once the currency exchange rate is taken into account.

Think about it: if you had two bonds with identical credit quality, maturity dates, and other characteristics, but A offered a higher real rate than B, bond investors would obviously pour money from B into A, quickly eliminating the difference.

For a US investor, a non-US bond is essentially the same as a domestic bond plus currency risk. The latter is an uncompensated risk, one with zero expected return. Since rule #1 in risk management is that you should never incur a risk you don't expect to get paid for, you should avoid foreign currency risk if you can.

Altogether, if you buy a foreign-currency bond and hedge out the currency risk, you'll end up with the same return as that of a domestic bond of comparable quality and duration, but you'll have paid more to buy the bond and to hedge the currency risk.

BOND FUNDS

You shouldn't buy individual issues of any bonds, with the possible exception of Treasuries. In particular, the muni-bond market is a cesspit of obscurantism, where retail investors are routinely scalped by salesmen promising "no commission" bargains, which have bid-ask spreads through which you could drive a double-wide.[xxxi] (For an explanation of bid-ask spreads see Glossary.) You might perhaps own individual muni-bonds in a well-diversified bond portfolio managed by an experienced expert who has access to wholesale pricing.

The rest of us should invest through bond funds, which hold many bonds. As I explain in the chapter on asset allocation, I don't think individual investors should own corporate bonds, even in a fund, except funds like Vanguard's Short-Term Bond Index Fund that hold short-term investment-grade corporates as a proxy for cash reserves. There's also no compelling reason to own non-US bond funds, since these are effectively foreign currency funds, and as such charge high fees for the privilege of speculating with your money.

As Jack Bogle and others have repeatedly documented, there's a perfect correlation between a bond fund's expense ratio (i.e., its total fees and expenses) and its return. In other words, the higher the fees, the worse the performance. Moreover, more expensive funds are more risky, because their managers have to reach for higher yield (which means lower quality) in order to compensate for the higher fees.

So in the perverse world of financial services, you pay more for a bond fund that will be more volatile and earn you less. How can this be? Why don't such funds go out of business?

Answer: Investor ignorance.

In the US bond markets, it's incredibly difficult for any investor (including professional bond fund managers) to gain an edge by being smarter than their peers at picking bonds—

except by taking on more risk, which eventually comes back to bite. So the rational choices for individual investors are plain vanilla no-load, low-cost bond index funds and ETFs, because these are the lowest cost options available.

Summary of Investing in Bonds

Should you invest in bonds? Probably yes.
If so, what kind?

- Treasuries.

- TIPS.

- Munis.

- Short-Term Investment Grade Corporates.

Don't invest in longer-term corporate bonds, whether investment grade or high-yield, nor foreign bonds, whether from developed or emerging markets.

How much? Depends entirely on your age, circumstances, investment plan and so forth—see the section on asset allocation in chapter 12.

And in what way?

- The only bonds you should ever buy directly are Treasuries.

• For all others invest in low-cost index funds or ETFs whenever possible.

• In bond funds and ETFs, the relationship between expense ratio and return is iron-clad: the bigger the expense ratio, the lower the return.

• Buy only low-cost bond funds.

CONCLUSION: STOCKS VERSUS BONDS

It's dangerously naïve to extrapolate historical returns on the assumption that the future will mirror the past; nevertheless, it's instructive to note that the worst 10-year real return for bonds has been about the same as that for stocks. Fundamentally, this is because stocks are a claim on real assets, whereas bonds pay only nominal returns, exposing them to the depredations of inflation.

In focusing only on the worst periods for stocks and bonds, we've ignored the distribution of relative performance over time:

• Stocks have outperformed bonds in 62% of all one-year periods since 1900.

• In 70% of all five-year periods.

- In 81% of all ten-year periods.

- And in 96% of all 25-year periods.

So stocks haven't always been the winner, but they should be the odds-on favorite over most periods of five years or longer.

This is why I can't agree with Jack Bogle's advice that an individual's allocation to bonds should be the same as his or her age.

Because none of us know how long we're going to live, we have to invest as if we'll make it to 100; we can't risk running out of money before we run out of time.

For the 65-year old retiree, this means an investment time horizon of 35 years. No one with that sort of time horizon should be 65% invested in bonds, especially today (mid-2013), when yields are at historical lows and investors are virtually guaranteed a negative real rate of return on their "safe" Treasury bond investments.

Part III

DON'T BELIEVE
WHAT THEY TELL
YOU ABOUT . . .

CHAPTER 4

Forecasts:
They're Worthless

Those who have knowledge don't predict. Those who predict don't have knowledge.

Lao Tzu

The only function of economic forecasting is to make astrology look respectable.

J.K. Galbraith

The reason that "guru" is such a popular word is because "charlatan" is so hard to spell.

William Bernstein

Yes, there are pundits and prognosticators galore: on CNBC; at Morgan Stanley, Goldman Sachs, J.P. Morgan, Merrill Lynch; in the newspapers, magazines, and journals; at colleges, think tanks, and universities; on the lecture circuit and in newsletter publications. But the dirty secret is that these experts' forecasts are no more accurate than flipping a coin.

They're not stupid and they're equipped with loads of data, computer analyses, sophisticated models, and so on. The problem is it can't be done. Or at least no one has yet figured out how to do it. And by "it" I mean the direction of the stock market, inflation, interest rates, corporate earnings, employment growth, GDP—I could keep going, but you get the picture.

If I had to pick just one piece of advice to shout to all investors it would be this:

The Key to Investment Success is Process, not Prognostication

Here's James Montier, an investment strategist with GMO in Boston, in *The Little Book of Behavioral Investing*:

The evidence on the folly of forecasting is overwhelming . . . We'll start . . . with the economists. These guys haven't got a clue. Frankly, the three blind mice have more credibility at seeing what is coming than any macro-forecaster. For instance, the consensus of economists has completely failed to predict any of the last four recessions (even once we were in them).[xxxii]

The analysts are no better. . . When an analyst first makes a forecast for a company's earnings two years prior to the actual event, they are on average wrong by a staggering 94 percent.

As for stock prices:

In 2008, the analysts forecasted a 24 percent price increase, yet stocks actually fell nearly 40 percent. In fact, between 2000 and 2008, the analysts hadn't even managed to get the direction of change in prices right in four out of nine years.[xxxiii]

Moreover, Montier rightly points out that "even if by some miracle of divine intervention your forecast turns out to be correct, you can only make money from it, if (and only if) it is different from the consensus." This is because the consensus is already reflected in today's stock prices, interest rates, and so on.

As Rick Ferri documents in his excellent book, *The Power of Passive Investing*, and on his website blog, the first thorough analysis of market forecasting prowess was undertaken by Alfred Cowles III in the 1930s. Cowles compiled approximately 7,500 market forecasts and stock picks from multiple sources between 1928 and 1932, and published the results in 1933. The forecasters' success rate was just over 35% and the average performance of the stock recommendations was 1.4% below that of the stock market as a whole.

As Ferri writes, "You would think today's analysts would do better given 80 more years of experience making forecasts, information and technology advancements, extensive financial disclosure by corporations and advanced analysis tools. Not so, according to CXO Advisory Group, an independent observer of Wall Street acumen."

With a compilation of 5,000 or so forecasts from about 60 different pundits in recent years, CXO reports a success rate of 33%, remarkably close to that reported by Cowles.[xxxiv]

The evidence on interest rates is no more encouraging. At the beginning and middle of each year, the *Wall Street Journal* polls leading Wall Street and academic economists for their forecasts of the yield on 10-year Treasury bonds in six months' time. In the 57 polls we have from 1982-2010,

64% of the forecasts were wrong about the direction of interest rates over the next six months. That's worse than flipping a coin.

(In fact, my colleague at Cambridge Associates who first published this research had a black lab named Guinness whose predictions on the direction of interest rates were 50% correct—substantially better than those of the experts. Guinness was planning to launch a hedge fund based on this sterling record, but alas he was called away to that great kennel in the sky before his SEC registration came through!)

So why are so many highly paid people employed to provide such forecasts? Good question. Two reasons: first, there's demand for them, despite the miserable track record. As investors, most people find the uncertainty inherent in financial markets simply intolerable. To accept this uncertainty is to acknowledge that we have no control over what might happen next, and, as psychologists tell us, we need to feel that we have some meaningful control over events. Savage sell-offs in the stock market strip such delusions—but not for long.

Second, prognostication, however flawed, gives the sales force a reason to call their customers and make sales. For example: "Our chief economist sees interest rates rising in the next six months as the economy improves, so our investment strategy team is recommending that we move some assets into shorter duration bonds to take advantage of this shift. Let's take profits in that bond fund you've held for the past few years, and invest the proceeds in a short-duration bond fund instead."

Sounds entirely reasonable, right? Assuming the chief economist is correct, which is a toss-up, and assuming the bond market behaves as predicted, which it might or might not, and assuming that taxes on realized gains and the sales commission on the new fund don't eat up any potential gains from the stars aligning exactly as forecast.

As J. Scott Armstrong of the Wharton School of Business puts it, "for every seer there is a sucker."[xxxv]

All intelligent, experienced, and honest forecasters are at pains to emphasize the low probability of their hitting the target. For example, Byron R. Wien, a veteran Wall Street pundit, is quoted in *The New York Times* as saying: "Few people get forecasts right very often. I certainly don't. I don't even attempt to make a literal forecast. I try to come up with some ideas that are provocative, and worth thinking about."

In the same article, (January 9, 2011), Aaron Gurwitz, the chief investment officer at Barclay's Wealth, stresses that "investment strategy is the practice of decision-making under uncertainty," and wishes his "friends and neighbors [would] stop asking me whether I think the stock market is going up or down."

So what's the lesson here? Well, don't hang your hat on any forecast, however authoritative the source; in fact, research has shown that the more prominent a forecaster and the greater his or her confidence, the worse the predictions. Since forecasts are notoriously inaccurate, it would be very risky to make any investment decision based on your conviction that such-and-such an outcome was assured.

Moreover, as Montier and others point out, this forecast

could already be reflected in stock and bond market prices—basically, you're too late.

Yet peering into the uncertain future is not a waste of time.

At Cambridge Associates, the research department's view of the markets is not driven by estimates of return, which they don't believe anyone can predict, but by an assessment of risk; that is, based on current market valuations relative to historical norms, do investors today seem unduly optimistic or pessimistic? If the former, risk is high (for long-term investors); if the latter, risk is low. Then they try to gauge how confident they are in their assessment, and in what ways and for what reasons they might be wrong. Finally, they try to evaluate the consequences of being wrong and how the risks that come with being wrong might be hedged out, if doing so seems worth the cost.

But even with all the relevant information, knowledge, and experience needed to work through this process, the end result is almost always flawed and incomplete. Getting the outlook more-or-less right is not enough—you must get the timing right too, otherwise your brilliant insights wither with every tick of the clock.

CONCLUSION

At the end of the day, individual investors should rely on just three predictions, which you can take right to the bank:

First: Over time equity markets revert to their long-term mean. This means that what has gone up a lot will eventually come back down and what has gone down a lot will eventually go back up. The way you should incorporate this prediction into your investment plan is by assiduous rebalancing.

Second: If you constantly adjust your investment portfolio in response to pundits' forecasts, you'll end up considerably poorer than if you ignore them all.

Third: If you consistently invest in higher-cost rather than in lower-cost investment products, you will line the pockets of investment managers at your own expense, with no commensurate gain in return.

CHAPTER 5

Market Timing Doesn't Pay

The perils of forecasting lead us directly to the dangers of market timing. This is the practice of diving into or out of the stock market—or significantly ratcheting up or down the amount you have invested in stocks—according to predictions of future stock market returns.

Because we all find it so difficult to accept that future stock market returns are unknown and unknowable, we're drawn to the siren song of market timing. Huge declines in market value, like those of 2000-2003 and 2008-2009, are so damaging and frightening that we naturally want to mitigate our exposure to such financial pain in the future. Market timing seems like a sensible way to limit our risk.

But here's the problem, or rather the problems:

First, forecasts are profoundly unreliable, as already discussed. So although long-term investors would realize considerable gains if they could avoid the stock market's worst months, who can predict which months those will be?

Exhibit 6
Market Timing: Missing the Worst Days

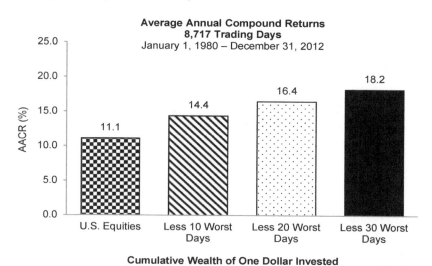

Average Annual Compound Returns
8,717 Trading Days
January 1, 1980 – December 31, 2012

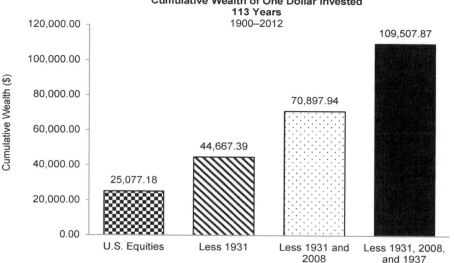

Cumulative Wealth of One Dollar Invested
113 Years
1900–2012

Secondly, each market timing decision is really two decisions: when to get out and when to get back in. Your chances of getting both those decisions consistently right are slim to none. The penalties for missing the stock market's best months are severe because stock market returns

Exhibit 7
Market Timing: Missing the Best Days

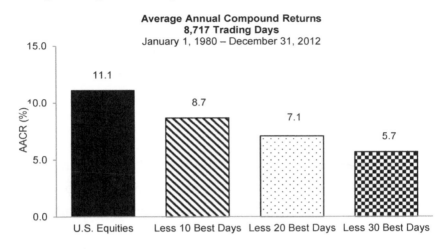

Average Annual Compound Returns
8,717 Trading Days
January 1, 1980 – December 31, 2012

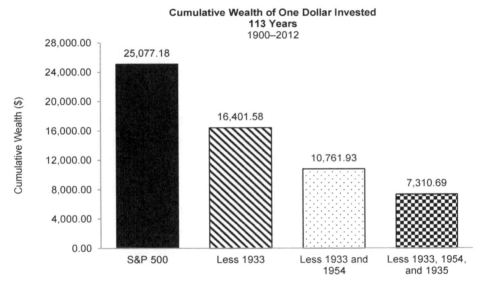

Cumulative Wealth of One Dollar Invested
113 Years
1900–2012

are highly concentrated in short bursts of time.

As these exhibits show, missing even a few crucial days, weeks, or months of stock market returns can have a devastating effect on your cumulative wealth over time. Consider this:

• If you had invested $100 in the US stock market on January 1, 1900, reinvested all dividends and remained fully invested through December 31, 2012, your $100 would be worth $80,177 even after adjusting for inflation (but ignoring taxes).

• There are 1356 months in this 113 year period. If you had missed the best 60 months out of those 1356—that is, just 4% of all the months—your cumulative real return on that $100 would be *zero*.

• In other words, you could have been invested in the US equity market 96% of the time during that 113 years, and earned absolutely nothing (after inflation).

Let's give Jack Bogle, the founder of Vanguard and tireless advocate for index investing, the last word on this topic:

The idea that a bell rings to signal when investors should get into and out of the stock market is simply not credible. After nearly 50 years in this business, I do not know of anybody who has done it successfully and consistently. I don't even know anybody who knows anybody who has done it successfully and consistently. [xxxvi]

CHAPTER 6

It's Not the Growth Rate, Stupid—It's the Price

POP QUIZ ON INVESTING IN GROWTH STOCKS

We have a secret crystal ball that tells us Dynamic Corp. is guaranteed to grow earnings at a compound average annual rate of 12% over the next 10 years.

And that HumDrum, Inc. is guaranteed to grow earnings at a compound average annual rate of 4% over the next 10 years.

Which company's stock would you rather buy today?

a) HumDrum (because this must be a trick question)
b) Dynamic (duh!)
c) No idea
d) I need more info to answer this question

You need more info to answer this question.

• It doesn't make any difference whether Dynamic Corp's earnings grow three times faster than those of HumDrum.

• What matters is the price you have to pay for those future earnings.

• That's what you're buying when you invest in a stock: a slice of the company's future earnings.

• For example, let's assume that Dynamic Corp is a hot stock (as Cisco Systems was in the late 1990s), and investors are currently assuming that it will grow earnings at 30% a year for the next 10 years and have priced the stock accordingly.

• If earnings growth comes in at "only" 12% a year (which, by the way, is excellent), then the stock price will be revalued downwards to reflect this lower-than-expected growth rate.

• Meanwhile, perhaps investors have pretty much written off HumDrum, Inc. and priced it accordingly (like Sears in 1999). But if rumors of HumDrum's demise prove premature and it revives to post a perfectly respectable 4% a year growth rate, its stock will rise considerably because it has *exceeded* investors' expectations.

What matters is *not* earnings, but the price paid for those earnings; and it's not so much the company's growth that matters, but investors' *expectations* for the company's growth.

Early in 2000, Cambridge Associates made a prediction about Cisco Systems, a very successful tech company, and Sears Roebuck, chosen as the epitome of a boring "old economy" company. We argued that expectations for Cisco's stock were so ludicrously high, and those for Sears so pessimistically low, that it was virtually certain that Sears' stock would outperform Cisco's in the next few years. Our objective wasn't to make stock recommendations, just to bang into our clients' heads how dangerously overvalued tech stocks had become.

In the next two-and-a-half years, Cisco's stock dropped 90%, from peak to trough, while Sears' stock rose 93%. Sears' sales and profits weren't particularly strong during this period; it's just that in their mad rush for all things tech, investors had totally neglected such stocks. After a few bad years, while the fallout from the tech bubble rattled earnings quite badly, Cisco returned to profitability. But it could never in 1,000 years realize the level of earnings investors had implicitly assumed when they bid the stock up to $81.44 and a stratospheric price-earnings multiple.

In *The Investor's Manifesto*, investment expert William Bernstein puts it this way:

> Good companies most often are bad stocks, and bad companies, as a group, are good stocks . . . the more public visibility a company has, and the more well-known and entertaining its story, the lower the future returns are likely

to be. By contrast, it is the most obscure and unglamorous businesses that often have the highest returns.[xxxvii]

Thus if you intend to buy individual stocks (which you probably shouldn't do, as discussed below) then there should be some reason for you to think that you have a special talent for assessing which companies' future earnings growth rates are currently underestimated by other investors—including, especially, the professional investors and their analysts, who dominate the market. Good luck with that.

Similarly, if you buy a growth stock fund, like those dot.com funds that flooded the market in 1999 and 2000, what you're buying is a slice of the future earnings of all the stocks owned by that fund. Again, what matters is not whether those companies' earnings grow fast, but whether they grow faster or slower than investors' expect.

The great British economist John Maynard Keynes gets the last word here:

"Successful investing is anticipating the anticipation of others."

GROWTH COUNTRIES

What applies to companies applies even more to countries. That is, how a country's growth rate is already priced is more relevant to investors than the growth rate itself.

In fact, as the following charts show, there is no historical correlation between a country's GDP growth and its stock market's return.

Exhibit 8
Real Economic Growth Rates and Stock Market Returns
1974–2012 • Local Currency

For any given time period, investors should not assume any correlation between a country's GDP growth and the performance of its stock market.

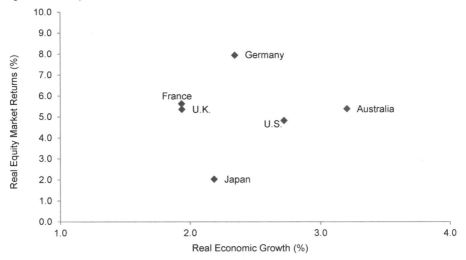

Exhibit 9
Real Economic Growth Rates and Stock Market Returns for Emerging Markets
1997–2011 • Local Currency

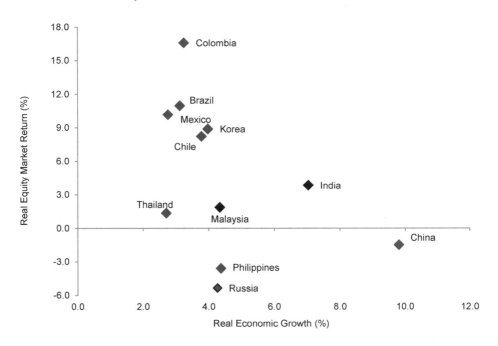

How can this be?

• Perhaps the composition of the stock market doesn't mirror that of the economy, so the two are disconnected (e.g., in Brazil, the stock market index is heavily skewed to natural resources). Remember, when you invest in stocks, you're investing in companies, not in the country.

• Perhaps the stock market is relatively immature and attracts only traders and gamblers because it lacks a solid institutional investment base (e.g., China).

• Perhaps dilution erodes stock market returns. In rapidly growing economies, public companies frequently dilute the value of existing investors' shares by issuing more and more shares to fuel their growth, damaging the stock price.

• Perhaps corporate governance is weak and investors lack confidence in the reliability of companies' earnings reports.

• Perhaps the most dynamic companies are private, family-owned businesses, and aren't listed on the stock market (e.g., Italy).

Perhaps . . . perhaps . . . perhaps.

Certainly, it helps investors if a country is growing steadily, its government is keen on encouraging the development of private enterprise and a robust stock market, and private businesses benefit from listing as public companies.

Nevertheless, do not assume that economic growth will be reflected in stock market returns. There are too many other variables at play, particularly whether over-optimistic expectations are already priced into the market.

The most comprehensive research on this topic came from Elroy Dimson, Paul Marsh, and Mike Staunton of the London Business School in the 2010 update of their annual *Credit Suisse Global Investment Returns Sourcebook.*

• Dimson, Marsh, and Staunton calculated that from 1972-2009, investors would have earned a return of 18.4% annually if they had invested each year in countries with the highest GDP growth rate over the preceding five years.

• But investing each year in those countries with the *lowest* GDP growth rate would have generated returns of 25.1% annually.

• Their conclusion? "Over the long run, there is not a positive association between a country's real growth in per capita GDP and the real returns from its stock market."

So when a broker or financial advisor of some sort recommends that you invest heavily in, for example, emerging markets because their prospective growth rates are higher than those of developed markets, you should just shake your head and turn a deaf ear.

Or point out that from 1988-2008, the US economy grew at an average annual rate of 2.8% and its stock market returned 8.8% a year. On the other hand, Thailand and Taiwan grew at 5.4% a year and their stock markets returned 4.4% and 3.8% respectively; Korea grew at an even better 5.6%, but its market returned just 4.9% a year; and China grew at a blistering rate of 9.6% a year while its equity market treated investors to an annualized return of -3.3%.[xxxviii]

As with companies, so with countries: investors wrongly assume that economic growth drives stock market returns, when the price you pay is really most important.

CHAPTER 7

Turn Off CNBC

Too often, much of the financial media are profoundly complicit in the dissemination of misinformation about investing. Their focus, understandably, is on daily (or even hourly) news, but this just encourages investors to think and behave in ways that damage their financial well-being.

Turn to the business section of any local or national newspaper and you'll probably find some sensible financial planning advice, some discussion of which sectors of the market look more or less attractive ("tech stock seem poised for a rebound") and some individual stock tips ("analysts say IBM could be an attractive pick for conservative investors"). These last two are useless twaddle. Worse than useless, because they distract us from what, as investors, we should actually be focused on: our long-term investment plan.

Moreover, the stock market report will comment on why the market did what it did yesterday; for example, "Renewed concern about the European debt crisis caused the market to sell off sharply yesterday." Also twaddle. We actually have no idea what motivated some participants in the stock market to sell yesterday and others to buy. As J.P. Morgan famously remarked, "the market will fluctuate." Within a range of ± 10% or so, stock market shifts are random, inexplicable, and, of course, entirely unpredictable. So these daily reports on the market are also misleading, with a misplaced focus on daily events. As investment author Charley Ellis says,

> *Investors should ignore that rascal Mr. Market and his constant jumping around. The daily changes in the market are no more important to a long-term investor than the daily weather is to a climatologist.*[xxxix]

All of this is ramped up dramatically, of course, on CNBC, Bloomberg TV, and other channels devoted to covering the markets. All those charts and graphs tracking hourly price changes of individual stocks and sectors; all those commentators and analysts and pundits—cut to the floor of the NYSE—cut back to the studio—cut to a reporter at the CBOE. It's fast, it's happening, it's exciting, it's where the action is. Then top it all off with the clowning antics of Jim Cramer (suitably excoriated by Yale's chief investment officer, David Swensen, in his book *Unconventional Success*), whose rantings are the verbal equivalent of toxic waste.

In their excellent short book, *The Investment Answer*, Daniel Goldie and Gordon Murray point out that

> *Wall Street brokers and the financial press would have you believe that investment results are mostly determined by*

how successful you are at: (1) timing when to get in and out of the market, (2) picking the right individual stocks and bonds to own, or (3) finding the next top-performing manager or mutual fund (or all of the above).[xl]

This advice is, of course, completely wrong on all three counts.

WHY DOES THE FINANCIAL PRESS DISSEMINATE SUCH DELUSIONS?

Follow the money! How do newspapers and television programs generate revenue? They sell subscriptions and ads. The more readers and viewers they have, the more of both they can sell at ever higher prices. So they're in the business of attracting and retaining readers and viewers, which they're unlikely to do if they report day after day that market fluctuations are largely random, that analysts' forecasts are worthless, that few individual investors should ever buy individual stocks, and that active managers generally don't beat the market.

Who buys the ads the media sell? Mostly financial service firms, like brokerage houses and mutual fund companies. Most of the media aren't about to bite the hand that feeds them. Besides, like all people, editors tend to follow the herd.

The brokers want you to be caught up in the action so

that you think you need to do something or other in response to the day's news. After all, they get paid when you transact—buy or sell, doesn't matter which—and so the shorter-term your attention span the better for them.

The mutual fund companies want you to believe that they can beat the market, despite voluminous evidence to the contrary. So they concentrate their advertising on whatever has done well recently, which encourages investors to buy high and sell low. David Swensen analyzed mutual fund advertisements in the quarterly mutual funds report published by the *Wall Street Journal* and concluded that

> *Every aspect of the Wall Street Journal's Mutual Funds Quarterly Review pushes the investing public in the wrong direction. The weight of the message increases as the attractiveness of the opportunity decreases. The focus on stocks peaks as stock prices peak. When bonds might prove most useful to investor portfolios, nary an advertisement mentions fixed income. The perversity of the mutual-fund industry's advertising rates a perfect ten.*[xli]

Similarly, in a 2012 article in the Georgia Law Review (46:2), "Mutual fund performance advertising: inherently and materially misleading?" professors Alan Palmiter and Ahmed Taha argue that

> *By implying that strong past performance will continue—the clear inference of reasonable investors—mutual fund*

companies use performance advertisements to engage in what one can describe only as a form of securities deception. . . . That is, mutual fund performance advertising violates securities antifraud standards. Additionally, these advertisements would be deceptive under FTC standards applicable to the advertising of other products and services.

So the steady babble of the financial media is mostly "noise" that you should switch off. By all means watch CNBC if you find it more entertaining than re-runs of CSI Miami, but beware of the seductive power of all that dynamic action. Both the implicit and explicit messaging is antithetical to sound investing.

GOLD NUGGETS IN THE SLUDGE

The first words of this chapter are "too often," and so what about the rest of the time? Anyone seriously interested in staying abreast of global economic and financial affairs on a daily basis should subscribe to the *Financial Times*, whose columnists are generally knowledgeable and insightful (*The Wall Street Journal* doesn't compete in this regard).

In addition to sound financial planning advice, the business section of main street papers occasionally offer excellent advice during times of stress. For example, after a week of wild gyrations in the stock market, Ron Lieber, writing in *The New York Times*, provided readers with very sensible advice to resist dumping stocks, remain invested in low-cost index funds, and

rebalance their investments back to long-term asset allocation targets.[xlii]

The following week *The New York Times* published a diatribe from David Swensen repeating the warnings given in
his book, *Unconventional Success*, that for-profit mutual fund
companies often exploit periods of market volatility to garner
profits from investors who are inveigled by salesmen into be-
lieving such funds offer a safe haven for their savings.

Similarly, Jason Zweig writes consistently intelligent,
informed commentaries in *The Wall Street Journal* that steer
investors in the right directions. Barry Ritholtz gives consistently sound advice in his "On Investing" column in *The
Washington Post*.

These examples illustrate the point that a wholesale indictment of the financial media is not warranted. Nevertheless, the fundamental problem remains: to attract readers and
viewers and sell the ads it depends upon for survival, the
media must find ways to hold our attention and interest, to
keep up the buzz, day after day, week after week. If you look
up Ron Lieber's article online, at www.nytimes.com, you'll
find the first page peppered with ads for online stock trading,
market timing services, penny stock investing, options trading, and other sure-fire losing propositions. Quite amusing,
in a perverse sort of way—as if an article promoting sexual
abstinence were surrounded by ads for condoms, male en-
hancement pills, testosterone booster shots, and so on.

Inevitably, the media's intense focus on what just hap-
pened results in its overstating the importance of recent

events and understating the significance of the longer historical perspective that's more relevant to most investors.

CONCLUSION

Those two highly experienced and sage investment experts, William Bernstein and Charley Ellis, give exactly the same sensible advice on this topic. Ellis writes,

> *Investing is not entertainment—it's a responsibility—and investing is not supposed to be fun or "interesting." It's a continuous process, like refining petroleum or manufacturing cookies, chemicals, or integrated circuits. If anything in the process is "interesting," it's almost surely wrong.*[xliii]

Bernstein's analogy is equally apt:

> *If it is excitement you seek, take up bungee jumping . . . If done properly, successful investing entertains as much as watching clothes tumble in the dryer window. Always remember that the more exciting a given stock or asset class is, the more likely it is to be over-owned, overpriced, and destined for low future returns.*[xliv]

CHAPTER 8

The Financial Services Industry Is Looking for You, Chump

Managing money is not the true business of the money management industry. Rather, it is gathering and retaining assets.

Goldman Sachs[xlv]

If doctors prescribed medicines to patients in the knowledge that they were more likely to do harm than good, and collected a commission for every drug they sold in this way, it would rightly be regarded as scandalous behaviour. When something similar happens in the fund business, nobody seems to blink an eyelid.

Jonathan Davis, *Financial Times*, 6/9/2008

A reliable way to make people believe in falsehoods is frequent repetition, because familiarity is not easily distinguished from truth. Authoritarian institutions and marketers have always known this fact.

Daniel Kahneman, *Thinking, Fast and Slow*

The financial services sector of the US economy is huge, employing millions of people and pervading all our lives in several ways. In fact, you probably know at least one person who works in financial services in some capacity. But for our purposes, we're only interested in those sub-sectors engaged in selling and managing investment products to and for individual investors.

This includes banks, keen to offer you the services of their "wealth management" division; "financial advisors" who offer investment management as part of their service; insurance reps who sell investment products (sometimes wrapped up with or in the guise of insurance products); stockbrokers (now called "investment consultants" or "financial advisors"); mutual fund companies, and independent investment advisors.

It's an amazing business: profit margins are huge by most industries' standards (which is why the world has over 70,000 investment funds of all sorts), and those working in the investment business are among the most highly compensated employees anywhere. Yet the industry consistently harms its clients.

An analysis commissioned by the IBM Institute for Business Value found that the global "fund management industry is destroying $1,300bn of value annually." That's $1.3 *trillion* dollars each year.[xlvi]

> *The bulk of the value destruction, almost $1,100bn a year . . . includes $300bn in excess fees for actively managed long-only funds that fail to beat their benchmarks . . . $250bn spent in fees for wealth management and ad-*

visory services that fail to deliver promised above-benchmark returns, and $51bn in fees for hedge funds that also fail to deliver their targeted returns.

Credit rating agencies, [Wall Street] research and trading are seen as destroying a further $459bn, largely due to the perceived inaccuracy of much of the analysis these sectors deliver.

The report argues the industry is destroying a further $213bn a year for shareholders due to organisational complexity, largely as a result of inefficiencies.

This value destruction is "unsustainable" in a world where . . . regulation is likely to become tighter in the wake of the financial crisis and investors are becoming more financially sophisticated, more price sensitive and increasingly keen to measure the "value-add" of their investment managers.

Wow! Read that again. How does such an industry survive, let alone thrive? Of course, most investors have never seen this report or even heard anything about it. Was it widely publicized in the financial media? Did you see it summarized on CNBC?

Nor is this an isolated analysis. In "The Cost of Active Investing," Ken French, a finance professor at Dartmouth's Tuck School of Business, estimates that in 2006 the cost of all forms of active management to all US stock market investors was $101.8 billion. "Thus, in 2006 investors searching for superior returns in the US stock market consume[d] more than 330 dollars in resources for every man, woman, and child in the United States."[xlvii] Where did this money go? To the financial services industry.

Similarly, a *New York Times* article recently estimated that US equity mutual funds alone raked in $46.9 billion in 2010,[xlviii] while Jack Bogle estimates the total mutual fund take at $69 billion.

Also highly unusual, compared to most businesses, is the way financial service firms constantly violate the laws and regulations governing their dealings with customers. Every other week seems to bring another news story like these:

• "J.P. Morgan agrees to $228m settlement" over a muni-bond price rigging scheme in which the firm "acknowledged illegal conduct by staff" (*Financial Times*, 7/8/2011).

• "Raymond James settles with SEC" for telling conservative clients that auction rate securities were a safe and secure investment. This was characterized by Florida's Office of Financial Regulation as "dishonest or unethical conduct" (*The Washington Post*, 6/30/2011).

• "Bank of America agrees to $14 billion toxic–mortgage payback" (*The Washington Post*, 6/30/2011)

• Wealthy customers accuse "Citicorp of fraud and breach of fiduciary duty, saying they had been misled about complex, risky investments that Citigroup had held out as safe and sound." (*The New York Times*, 1/14/2012).

And, of course, I could go on and on and on in this vein.[xlix]

With its takeover of Merrill Lynch, Bank of America's private banking division is one of the largest asset managers in the world, managing almost $2 trillion for clients. This despite Merrill's terrible track record: the bankruptcy of Orange County, California in 1994 as a result of Merrill Lynch's advice; the huge losses clients suffered in newly-minted tech funds launched at the very top of the dot.com bubble; the $50 billion it vaporized in the credit crisis.

But it has long been the case that most investment products are *sold* rather than bought. In other words, most transactions are initiated by someone with a financial incentive to make a sale, not by investors acting on their own initiative—although the dramatic increase in assets invested in low-cost index funds suggests that more and more investors are wising up.

THE PROBLEM IS SIMPLE: CONFLICT OF INTEREST

The financial interests and incentives of investment managers (including mutual funds) should be aligned as closely as possible with those of their clients.

But usually they're not. The investment management firms all say that their clients' interests always come first. This is simply not true, nor should it be true. The first loyalty of a public company must be to its shareholders. *Their* interests should always come first.[1]

Which sets up a classic principal-agent conflict of interest. Whatever rhetoric is disseminated for public consumption, job one for these firms and their employees is making money for themselves and for their shareholders. This is no different than at any other public company, and any client who fails to understand this is naive.[li]

Has the investment management industry succeeded in making lots of money for its clients as well as for itself? No. Far from it. As reported in the IBM-sponsored study cited above, the global investment management industry does *not* add value for its clients—it never has and there's absolutely no reason to think it ever will. On the contrary, its clients suffer the double whammy of paying high fees and then failing to earn returns that match those of widely-available, much cheaper alternatives.

In a May 1, 1997 speech to the Investment Company Institute (a trade organization for the mutual fund industry), Jason Zweig posed this question to his audience: "Are you primarily a marketing firm, or are you primarily an investment firm? You can be mostly one, or you can be mostly the other, but you cannot be both in equal measure."[lii] Then Jason succinctly outlined what differentiates a marketing firm from an investment firm. Unfortunately, the intervening years have made it eminently clear that the executives in his audience almost universally chose the marketing route.

Abetted by the financial media, the majority of firms offering investment management services work hard to seduce investors into behaving in ways that generate profits for the firms, but are detrimental to investors' financial well-being. The evidence is then obfuscated by inadequate performance reports.

In short, much of the industry strives to transfer money from the gullible to the larcenous and then cover up the crime.

WHO ARE THESE PEOPLE?

In the investment business there are, have been, and always will be total sleaze-bags running pump-and-dump bucket shops,[liii] Ponzi schemes, and all manner of similar scams and frauds.[liv] The potential rewards are so great, the supply of gullible suckers so infinite, the wheels of SEC regulatory enforcement so cumbersome.

But the vast majority of employees in the investment management industry are no different from those in any other business. They work hard, do the best they can for their boss, their firm, their clients and customers. They try to get ahead and make a good living. The salesmen and women (or "financial advisors") on the front line—those dealing directly with clients to whom they provide investment advice and recommend investment products—are impossibly conflicted. Most realize this but rationalize it away. Typically they have no objective means of measuring how well or badly their clients' portfolios are doing, because the statements their firms provide don't show their clients' performance compared to that of the markets in which they are invested (see chapter 14, "Keeping Score").

Of course, some financial service firm employees see their job as simply selling as much as possible of whatever products generate the highest payout to them personally, and damn the customers. At some shops, this is the pervasive culture. Mutual fund companies are notorious for launching new funds to capitalize on investors' propensity to chase hot sectors; for example, in 2000, when Cambridge Associates' research was characterizing the technology sector as a "dangerous bubble," 84 technology stock funds were introduced just in time for the dot.com bust.

Nevertheless, most financial advisors do their best to cultivate long-term relationships with clients, providing them with products and services the advisors believe will serve their clients' needs. Unfortunately, the compensation structure at most financial service firms actually *precludes* their giving clients suitable advice and transfers money from investors to the advisory firms *with no commensurate value-added*. As noted above, neither the clients nor their advisors are generally aware of this because no one is keeping score properly.

In fact, financial insult is added to financial injury when investors pay higher costs for products that are likely to deliver inferior returns. And our society as a whole is damaged by this, through lower returns on retirement savings that have been diverted, in effect, into the pockets of those who claim to be serving investors' best interests.

CONCLUSION

Most employees in the financial services industry who provide investment advice are compensated by commissions on products they sell to their clients or by fees from wrap accounts (see the discussion of wrap accounts in chapter 11). The prevalence of this practice does not legitimize it. Rather, it ensures that the financial interests of the advisors are in conflict with those of their clients, which is plain wrong.

Indeed, this is precisely why regulators around the world are looking to ban sales incentives for financial advisors. As Robert Pozen and Theresa Hamacher report in their *Financial Times* article, "Regulators ban fees and conflicts," (9/9/2013), "Bans are already in place for at least some products in Australia, the Netherlands and the UK. . . . [These] eliminate incentives for advisers to choose products with high payouts to advisers, even when a lower-fee option might be better for their clients."

This does *not* mean that all commission-earning advisors are mercenary predators, not at all—most are as ethical and honest as their position allows. But that's my point: *their position does not allow them to act in their clients' best interests*, since that would entail advising clients to invest in products that paid no commission although they had, in fact, a higher probability of helping clients' realize their investment objectives.

Consequently, as a saver and investor, a good rule of thumb is that you should never transact with any investment advisor, broker, financial planner, insurance agent and so on whose income is derived, in whole or in part, from wrap-account fees or commissions on product sales.[lv]

Are there no exceptions, ever? Well, sure—as with any rule of thumb, this isn't an absolute prohibition. But you really should have a very compelling reason for dealing with someone compensated in that way, and if you do so, you should understand very clearly what costs you are incurring— not just in commissions and/or fees, but also in opportunity cost; that is, what you *could* have earned had you invested in lower-cost, passively managed index products.

Before you shrug off this advice because you've dealt with Joe or Susan or Peter for years and have a good relationship, ask yourself: do I *really* know what investing with Joe's firm has cost me over the years? If not, read chapter 11, "Costs Matter Far More Than You Think."

For a final word on this topic, here is Professor Teresa Ghilarducci of the New School for Social Research, writing in *The New York Times* (July 21, 2012):

> *In my ad hoc retirement talks, I repeatedly hear about the "guy." This is a for-profit investment adviser, often described as, "I have this guy who is pretty good, he always calls, doesn't push me into investments." When I ask how much the "guy" costs, or if the guy has fiduciary loyalty— to the client, not the firm—or if their investments do better than a standard low-fee benchmark [i.e., index fund], they invariably don't know."*

And when it comes to investing, what you don't know can cost you plenty.

So wise up, chump. Those tickets your "guy" at Raymond James gave you for the Eagles-Giants game or the great hospitality you enjoyed at the UBS pavilion at the US Open golf tournament—who do you think is paying for all that?

CHAPTER 9

Active Fund Management: There's No Value Added

WHAT IS "ACTIVE" INVESTING?

When you invest in stocks or bonds, you can do so either through passive index funds that simply own (or replicate) all or part of the total stock or bond market, or through "active" managers that attempt to outperform the market return and charge relatively high fees. If you hire the latter, you are incurring "active risk": the risk that your active managers' returns turn out to be less than those of the market, despite high fees.

Investors should never take risks that they are unlikely to get paid for and that they can avoid. Active risk meets both these criteria; that is, you're not likely to get paid for taking this risk, since most active managers underperform, and you can avoid this uncompensated risk simply by investing in low-cost index funds.

The stock market's return is the composite return of all investors in the stock market; consequently, for some investors to outperform the stock market, some other investors must underperform. In other words, there's only one pie and if I manage to get a bigger-than-average slice, someone else's slice must be smaller. It's a zero-sum game where the winners win at the expense of the losers. Historically, the biggest losers—the patsies—have been individual investors like you and me.

So the notion that most managers can beat the market is logically impossible. In fact, since managers charge management fees and incur investment expenses, the average manager *must* underperform the market return (net of fees and expenses) by whatever amount those fees and expenses add up to.

This is exactly what multiple studies of active management have shown: the average fund manager underperforms the market by about 1.5% (or 150 basis points), about equal to average fees and expenses.

Moreover, most active stock and bond fund managers run relatively diversified portfolios in order to manage risk—quite rightly so. But this means that much of what they own will also be included in whatever index serves as appropriate benchmark they're trying to beat.

If you are considering investing in, say, a large-cap US stock fund, wouldn't you want to know how much of what it owned was already in the S&P 500 and what wasn't? Since you can buy the part that is the same at a cost of 9 basis points by investing in the i-Shares S&P 500 Index ETF, it doesn't make sense to pay an active manager 100 basis points more just to hold the same shares. In other words:

• 100% of the active manager's value added needs to come from the parts of his portfolio that are *different* from the index.

• That part needs to outperform the index by more than enough to pay for the additional fees levied by active managers.

• So if, for example, US Equity Fund A has an expense ratio of 109 basis points (i.e., 1.09%), and its holdings overlap 75% with those of the S&P 500, then the 25% of Equity Fund A that is different from the S&P 500 must outperform the index by more than 400 basis points for the fund as whole to generate a better return than I could earn investing in the i-Shares S&P500 ETF at a cost of 9 basis points.

• And 400 basis points is huge. It would be quite extraordinary for any manager to achieve this degree of outperformance in large-cap US equities over time. Thirty or 40 years ago, perhaps. Today and in the future? Most unlikely.

A Venn diagram, showing two portfolios that overlap, illustrates this issue.

ACTIVE PORTFOLIO MANAGEMENT

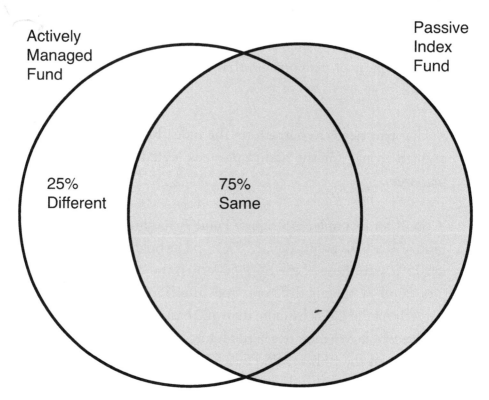

Obviously, the part of the active manager's portfolio that consists of the same stocks as those in the index will earn the same return. Now if Exxon comprises 2% of the manager's portfolio, and 3.7% of the S&P 500 index, then only 2% of Exxon will be in the "Same" space, and the 1.7% difference will be in the "Different" space. So it's not just a question of whether the manager owns the same stocks as those in the index, but also of whether he owns more or less of them than the index does.

The bottom line is that whatever part of the manager's portfolio overlaps necessarily earns the same returns as that part of the index with which it overlaps, and so 100% of any outperformance must come from the part that is different. Since the manager's fees and expenses are calculated as a percentage of the whole portfolio, not just the part that's different from the index, the part that's different must outperform by a lot just to make up for these costs.

This can apply to the market as a whole, or a subset like small-cap stocks. One can also buy a small-cap index return relatively cheaply.

Actively managed mutual funds should charge two fees: a small fee for whatever portion of the return comes from simply being invested in the market—which we can determine by calculating the overlap with a suitable index--and a performance fee based on any returns over and above those of the market. But don't hold your breath!

A manager could, of course, run a highly concentrated portfolio of only 10 or 15 stocks—and some managers of institutional equity portfolios do just that. But this adds risk—for both the investors and for the manager's business—and almost no mutual fund company managing money for individual investors would take such a business risk. Research has shown that mutual funds running concentrated portfolios of this sort have historically performed even worse than more diversified, actively managed funds.

More risk, less return. Not a winning formula.

CAN YOU PICK THE WINNERS AND AVOID THE LOSERS?

As with any distribution around an average, some managers must be above the average and some below. Again, numerous studies have shown that in any given period of one, three or five years, about 1/3 of active stock fund managers do better than the stock market and 2/3 do worse.

The problem is that the 1/3 that does better doesn't stay the same. Maybe some do better for three or four years, but inevitably they subsequently do worse. Indeed, doing better than average for several years is often a prescription for doing worse in the following years, because managers who have done particularly well are usually flooded with money from investors eager to profit from their success.[lvi] But as any responsible manager will attest, it's much harder to manage $20 billion than to manage $5 billion, especially if your investment niche is, say, small-cap stocks.

Obviously we can easily identify the 1/3 of managers who outperformed over the last three or five or 10 years. But since there is no reason whatsoever to extrapolate from this data the expectation that these same managers will continue to outperform in the future (indeed, rather the opposite, if history is any guide), how can we select the *future* winners?

Well, this is very difficult and frankly, for individual investors, a mug's game. There's overwhelming evidence that most investors have no better chance than a blind squirrel at identifying those fund managers who will outperform the market over the next three, five or 10 years.

There's also overwhelming evidence that because the financial services industry encourages everyone to chase after yesterday's winners, investors consistently earn poor returns by paying active management fees for subpar performance.

I could fill page after page with citations of and quotations from the massive volume of literature that has accumulated over the decades on both these topics: the underperformance of active fund managers and the virtual impossibility of identifying in advance which funds might be among the top third to outperform over the next one, three or five years.[lvii] Over 80 years, since the first research on this topic was published in the mid-1930s, every independent study of whatever period, with whatever data set, has produced the same conclusions.

Rick Ferri's *The Power of Passive Investing* has a useful review of the historical literature on the subject. Larry Swedroe's *The Quest for Alpha* summarizes the same research. Of course Jack Bogle, in his *Common Sense on Mutual Funds* and in many other publications dating back to his original work in the 1970s, has done extensive analyses of active management, arriving at the same conclusions.

It gets worse: active risk compounds when one constructs a portfolio of several active managers. Rick Ferri explains:

> *A portfolio of several actively managed funds has lower odds of success than each fund independently. As more actively managed mutual funds are added to a portfolio, the outperformance rate for the total portfolio drops dramatically. This problem compounds over time, and after enough*

time, the probability for outperforming a passive approach drops to near 0 percent.[lviii]

How come? Three reasons:

• First, 2/3 of active managers will underperform in any given period.

• Second, we can't tell in advance which managers will be among the 1/3 who outperform.

• Third, the managers who underperform do so by a larger margin, 1.6 percentage points on average, than the margin of outperformance of the winners, which averages 0.6 percentage points.

So let's imagine that you have a large leather bag full of marbles, and 2/3 of them are red and 1/3 green. You have to draw marbles from the bag without looking inside.

• Every time you pick a green marble, you get somewhere from 10 cents to $1.50, with an average payout of 60 cents.

• Every time you pick a red marble, you have to pony up anywhere from 10 cents to $2.50, with an average payment of $1.60.

You see where this is going, right? Not only is the deck stacked against you because most of the marbles are red, but over time you're also going to lose more on the average red marble than you win on each green. What will happen eventually? Well, obviously you'll eventually go broke—unless you quit playing.

The reason most investors continue to play this game is because they are repeatedly sold and severely infected by two delusions:

1. If a fund performed well in recent years it will perform well in future years. Extensive objective research has proved that this statement is demonstrably false.

2. We—or our financial advisor—can predict which actively managed funds will perform better and which will perform worse in future years. Extensive objective research has proved that this statement is also demonstrably false.

So you should follow the advice given again and again and again by all the disinterested experts who have written on this subject: quit playing the high cost, active risk game where the deck is doubly stacked against you, and buy index funds instead, where you *know* you will earn the return of the stock or bond market and not incur the risk of underperformance. Investing is difficult and risky enough without increasing your chances of failing to meet your goals by taking on a risk that history tells us you're not going to get paid for.

MARKET "EFFICIENCY"

A market is considered "efficient" if all investors have equal access to all the information required to determine fair market value. Under these conditions, if a stock—or an entire stock market—deviates from its fair market value, then investors recognizing this will almost immediately buy or sell it, bringing the price back to the "correct" value.

Two conclusions follow from this thesis: the first is that stock prices are inherently unpredictable (an idea first explored in the mid-nineteenth century), and the second is that investors can't consistently outperform the market (on a risk-adjusted basis).

The academic version of this is known as the Efficient Market Hypothesis (EMH), which was developed by Eugene Fama at the University of Chicago in the 1960s. Although always controversial, EMH was the academic orthodoxy until challenged in the 1990s by behavioral finance research.

EMH was always somewhat wacky, because it assumed that all investors had equal access to all relevant information and were rational automatons who interpreted this information in the same way. Of course, individual investors have nothing like the resources to enable them equal access to all relevant information—I don't have a Bloomberg machine on my desk, do you? Secondly, we've always known that investors are driven by successive waves of fear and greed, which leads them to entirely irrational, emotional decisions having nothing whatsoever to do with "intrinsic value."

Moreover, as John Kay recently noted, "A contradiction lies at the heart of the efficient market hypothesis: if efficient market prices did incorporate all available information about the value of an asset, no one would have an incentive to obtain that information in the first place." (*Financial Times*, 7/17/2013).

Then, of course, there's the Warren Buffett factor, which goes like this: "If the stock market is so efficient, how come Warren Buffett has managed to beat it like a drum for decades on end?" Nor can EMH readily explain how markets are subject to sudden crashes, like that of October 19, 1987, when the US stock market dropped 20% in one day.

For these reasons, active fund managers have little trouble pouring scorn on EMH (which challenges the notion that they can beat the market through market timing or stock picking acumen). But this is tilting at windmills. It's designed to divert your attention from the incontrovertible, uncomfortable, and persistent truth that in any given period, two-thirds of active managers fail to outperform whatever benchmark index is their relevant yardstick, and that no-one has yet devised any method of determining which managers will be in that one-third of winners in future periods.

A market doesn't need to be completely efficient for most active managers to fail. It only needs to be pretty efficient, just enough so that by the time you take fees and expenses into account, active managers struggle against a fierce headwind that few can overcome. With almost 75% of all US stocks held by institutional investors, the competition in this zero-sum contest is largely among well-resourced, highly trained professionals. This is a different world from that of, say, 1980, when individual investors owned about 65% of the US equity market.

So, yes, investors are frequently irrational, and both individual stocks and the stock market as a whole are subject to crazy gyrations. For example, there was nothing rational or "efficient" about the spike in the stock price of companies that changed their names to something.com in the late 1990s—without changing their business. Nevertheless, all the evidence indicates that the US market is efficient enough most of the time that active retail fund managers will continue to disappoint investors who have paid them substantial fees and received less than nothing in return.

AREN'T THERE ANY WINNERS?

Yes, of course there are active managers who have outperformed both the market and their competitors. As noted above, whenever you have a large distribution around an average of anything, some results are going to be above and some below that average. If you have such a manager in your portfolio, congratulations—you're one of the lucky ones.

I use the word "lucky" advisedly—after all, every day thousands of punters walk out of Las Vegas casinos with broad smiles on their faces because they've won. Thousands. Every day. But would you bet on their winning tomorrow?

So if you're invested with an active manager who's outperformed the market (net of fees, expenses and taxes on realized gains) over a long period of time, you're a lucky winner. Not an investment genius (sorry!), just lucky.

If you have deep, professional knowledge of the universe of active investment managers, you can shrink the odds of failure—just as a truly skillful blackjack player can narrow the odds against him at Vegas. But you also need to devote the time and resources to get that knowledge.

Sixteen years ago, when I was in charge of investment manager research at Cambridge Associates, I had the expertise, the time, and the resources to focus on identifying active managers I thought likely to generate superior returns for our institutional clients. The results were a mixed bag.

It was obvious from our analysis that US equity manager returns were quite cyclical, because sometimes smaller-cap stocks would do better than large-cap for a few years, or so-called value stocks would do better than growth stock—and then the worm would turn and the opposite would be true for the next few years.

But we found it very difficult to persuade clients to invest with good managers whose returns in recent years had been sub-par, which is exactly when one should invest with them.

As an individual investor, I know the odds are heavily stacked against me. Many of the best US equity managers don't manage retail funds available to individual investors. The fees and expenses for almost all retail funds are significantly higher than for funds available only to institutions. I don't have ready access to the data needed to conduct proper due diligence. And it's very unlikely that managers will agree to meet me so that I can judge how capable they really are. And . . . and . . . and. I could go on, but the point is that when I had the time, resources, expertise, and ability to meet managers face-to-face, plus lower fee schedules—all the advantages individual investors lack—the odds of my identifying US equity managers who'd outperform over the next five years were still marginal.

Superior non-US equity managers proved easier to identify. This is because overseas stock markets were (and still are) less efficient than the US market. Managers focused on finding undervalued stocks (i.e., value managers) consistently outperformed. In addition, the opportunity set was more diverse, encompassing European, Asian and emerging market companies.

However, for retail investors the higher costs of non-US equity funds generally negates any value added by active managers.

That's why most of my own equity investments are in index funds.

WHAT ABOUT WEALTH MANAGEMENT FIRMS?

Affluent investors with $1 million or more often entrust their assets to the "private bank" or "wealth management" division of large firms like UBS, Wells Fargo, Northern Trust, Bank of America, Morgan Stanley, J.P. Morgan, PNC Financial, Citicorp, and so on. One would assume that they'd pay substantially less in fees than the rest of us. Not so.

According to a *Financial Times* article of July 13, 2011, "Managers struggle to woo the wealthy," fees typically run from 2% to 3%, which presents the investment managers at these firms with an almost insuperable hurdle in their efforts to perform at least in line with the markets. Not surprisingly, these firms have been struggling to retain clients, who are defecting in disillusioned droves.

Performance data are hard to come by, because the firms don't release this information and obfuscate the issue by saying that "each client has unique needs," and so on. Of course, the lack of such data is very telling—do you think they'd be shy about releasing market-beating results?

Moreover, the data researchers have obtained indicate that, no, net of fees and taxes, these wealth management firms do not outperform market indexes--whether they manage clients' money in-house or hire external managers. The US stock and bond markets are particularly difficult to beat, non-US stock and bond markets somewhat less so, but the same logic applies across the board: why incur the additional costs and risks inherent in active management when the odds are firmly against your being rewarded for doing so?

CONCLUSION

Most investors simply don't know that decades of research have produced a mountain of evidence indicting active management as a waste of money. On the other side of the coin, there's a massive industry dedicated to denial and obfuscation, encouraging you to take active risk, because they (not you) get paid very handsomely for diverting your money into the hands of active managers.

But you need to wake up and smell the coffee: by all means play golf with your friends who are stockbrokers, financial advisors, insurance agents, and so on, but do not give them your money to invest. Frankly, many of them are ignorant of the damage they're doing to their customers and clients when they sell them expensive, actively managed mutual funds. Their employers certainly don't educate them on this subject. Nor do they track performance in a way that would reveal

1. How much of investors' returns are diverted into managers' pockets and

2. How badly they are doing, net of fees and taxes, relative to how they could have done investing the same amount in low-cost index funds or ETFs.

The smart alternative is very simple—and dramatically simplifies your investment decision-making. Incur as little active risk as possible, investing mostly in passively managed, low-cost stock or bond market index funds.

HIRING AND FIRING ACTIVE MANAGERS

At Cambridge Associates, we always worried that our institutional clients were too quick to fire managers that were underperforming. Over many years, working with many clients, we noticed that most seemed to accept that one year was too short a time period to judge an active manager's performance. But if the manager underperformed over two years, clients generally became antsy, and after three years they fired the bum.

Our view was that clients should exercise far greater care hiring active managers, and should hire only those to whom they would be happy giving more money if they underperformed. In other words, the clients should rebalance among their managers, taking money away from those that had done particularly well and giving it to those that had performed poorly. Why? Because manager performance tends to be cyclical, not linear. Far too few clients followed this advice.

So we created this exhibit to hammer home our point. The managers shown here manage three types of large-cap US stock portfolios for institutional investors: large-cap growth, large-cap value, and large-cap diversified (i.e., "core" portfolios). We picked those managers in each category whose performance over the past ten years (April 1,

2002 – March 31, 2012) was top quartile; that is, the best 25% of their peer group. Then we asked the question: what percentage of these top-performing managers had returns over at least one 36 month period during this ten years that put them in the bottom half, and bottom quartile, of their peer group?

When you look at this table, remember, we have prese-lected the 10-year *winners* here.

DO WINNING US EQUITY MANAGERS ALWAYS WIN?

Of those large-cap US equity managers in the top quartile for the past decade, what percentage had below average performance during at least one three-year stretch?

	% in bottom 50%	% in bottom 25%
Growth Managers	89%	57%
Value Managers	82%	57%
Diversified Managers	100%	79%

What's the point? Well, the point is that the winners sometimes look like losers. In every category, most of these winning managers spent at least 36 months, at some point in the decade, in the bottom 25% of the pack. At which point many of the investment committees we advised would run out of patience and fire them. So even successful managers are never successful in every period. This is because every investment management firm has a particular style or bias or method that it sticks to. Even if that style or bias or method succeeds in generating market-beating results over the long term (and most don't), there will certainly be periods—sometimes quite long periods—when it's out of synch with whatever is doing best in the market, resulting in relatively poor returns.

CONCLUSION

As I've already noted, it's extremely difficult to figure out which managers might prove the best over the next ten years (since historical data tell us they're not those who did best in the past ten years).

And this analysis shows that even if you were to succeed in picking managers that came out in the top 25% over the next ten years, chances are they'd spend at least one three-year period during that decade in the bottom half of the performance table.

When you might very well fire them.

WHY NOT PICK STOCKS?

Many investors—especially older investors—equate stock market investing with picking stocks. Years ago, that's how most savers invested in stocks: they had an account at Merrill Lynch or Dean Witter or E.F. Hutton and weighed the advice of their stockbroker as to which stocks and bonds to buy and sell.

Every analysis of such accounts has shown that the vast majority of these investors' portfolios underperformed the market as a whole. The few that outperformed were just lucky. In other words, almost everyone would have been far better off investing in stocks through a passive index fund. But such funds weren't around in the 1950s and 1960s, and were barely known and understood until the late 1980s. Even then, most investments in the growing number of mutual funds were by investors who had been sold an actively managed fund that paid the selling broker a commission. Meanwhile, many investors continued to construct portfolios of individual stocks.

And why not? For many people, picking stocks is an intriguing challenge. Perhaps they subscribe to *Value Line* or a similar service designed to help identify smart picks. The problem is what's called market efficiency. A stock market is "efficient" if every investor, whether individual or institutional, has access to all publicly available information about a company at the same time. Securities and Exchange regulations are designed to ensure this is the case; if you trade on "inside" information—that is, information not made publicly available—you can be sent to jail.

The US stock market is very efficient. Because the vast majority of stocks are now bought and sold by institutional investors, not by individuals, every single one of the 6,700 or so stocks in the US market is pored over constantly by armies of money managers (from hedge funds, pension funds, retail mutual funds, and so on) in an exhaustive effort to identify stocks that will generate market-beating returns. But as I keep stressing, it's a zero-sum game. The total aggregate return of all these investors is the market return (minus whatever costs they incur), and so the winners win at the expense of the losers.

As an individual investor, this is your competition. Do you stand on the loading dock of XYZ corporation counting the number of widgets they're shipping this month? Do you have a computer program that tracks the price momentum of every stock in, say, the Russell 3000 index, to identify those that seem to be attracting increased numbers of buyers? Can you tell when that momentum will peak and reverse? What special knowledge or skill do you have that will enable you to identify undervalued stocks before others have done so? What about growth stocks? Remember, good, strong, rapidly growing companies very often make lousy stock picks. Why? Because such companies attract over-optimistic investors whose buying pushes the stock price into nosebleed territory. If you analyze which kind of stocks have performed best over time, you'll find that sexy, small-cap growth stocks have been the worst sector of the market, while boring, dividend-paying, large-cap value stocks have done best.

What about those great tech stocks that led the computer revolution? Hewlett Packard, Microsoft, Apple, Google? It's pretty easy to pick winners after the race is over. What about Commodore International, Wang Labs, Atari? Don't recognize those names? They're all computer pioneers that went bust. Apple, which became the largest company in the world by market capitalization, was almost bankrupt before the second coming of Steve Jobs resurrected the brand.

By all means have fun picking stocks, if that's your idea of fun. Of course, if you really do know more about a particular industry than almost anyone else because you've worked in it for decades, you might actually have a real edge over the professional investors. But please use only a very small portion of your savings to indulge in this hobby and invest the rest more wisely. And keep score. If you're going to play, you should track whether you're winning or losing.

That applies to kids too. I think it's a great idea to encourage your children to learn something about saving and investing by giving them $1,000 to invest in stocks they research and select themselves. Think of it as tuition money.

But they should also keep score properly so that they learn what it means to compete with the pros in a zero-sum game.

You can simplify scorekeeping by running a paper portfolio parallel to your actual stock portfolio. Every time you buy a stock, pretend you've invested the same amount of money in an appropriate Vanguard or Fidelity or Schwab index fund or ETF (e.g., large-cap growth stock index, or small-cap value index, depending on the kind of stock you've bought). This way, you can easily figure out for any given period whether you've done better or worse, net of costs and taxes on gains, than if you had invested in these passive index funds.

In this contest, in the long run, my money's on those index funds!

CHAPTER 10

Not All Passive Investments Are the Same

Despite the best efforts of financial service firms and mutual fund companies, more and more investors have learned that it rarely pays to invest with active managers, and have chosen instead to invest in passive index funds. However, there is no such thing as *totally* passive investment because you simply can't buy every stock or every bond in the world, nor can any investment manager.

The closest you can get to a completely passive stock market investment is Vanguard's Total World Stock Index Fund. Even if we consider only domestic markets, a decision to invest in an S&P 500 Index fund or a Russell 3000 Index fund or a Dow Jones Wilshire 5000 Index fund is an active decision, because each of these is a slightly different version of the US stock market. (The Wilshire 5000 is the most comprehensive of the three; the S&P 500 Index covers only 85% of the total US stock market.)

Then you can take a further step along the passive-to-active spectrum by deciding to invest in, say, the Russell 1000 Value index, perhaps because you believe that over the long haul value investing (buying stocks that sell at lower valuations than most) will outperform growth-stock investing (buying stocks of companies with faster growth rates than average). The DFA funds, referred to in chapter 1, are relatively low-cost index funds with a slight tilt towards value stocks and smaller-capitalization stocks, since academic research has shown that over time this approach adds value—and so it has at DFA. Or you might refine your value tilt by selecting an index fund or exchange-traded fund (ETF) comprised of stocks of companies with better-than-average dividend yield.

In other words, there are many passive index funds one can choose from, and that choice is necessarily an active investment decision.

What differentiates this from investing in an actively managed fund, however, is that the passive fund has no manager trying to pick stocks that will outperform. Whatever the sector—large-cap, mid-cap, small-cap, value, core or growth—a passive fund simply holds all the stocks in that sector, usually weighted according to their relative capitalization, and so will perform exactly in line with the performance of that sector, minus the relatively small fee such funds typically charge. Transactions occur only when a stock moves in or out of the index your fund tracks. So, for example, when Standard and Poor's dropped Cephalon from the S&P 500 index (because it was being bought by another company) and added TE Connectivity in its place (on October 14, 2011), S&P 500 index funds had to follow suit. This low turnover of stocks in the index makes index funds relatively tax-efficient.

But beware: not all "passive" investments are created

equal. In fact, seeing customers defect to index funds, some brokerage firms decided that if they couldn't beat 'em they should join 'em, and added index funds to their mutual fund roster. For example, J.P. Morgan's Equity Index fund "seeks investment results that correspond to the aggregate price and dividend performance of securities in the Standard & Poor's 500 Composite Stock Price Index (S&P 500 Index)." Total annual operating expenses (the expense ratio) are 0.96%. However, there is also a sales charge, presumably scaled according to how much one invests, which maxes out at 5.25%.

Fidelity's no-load S&P 500 Index fund has an expense ratio of 10 basis points (0.10%)—or 7 basis points (0.07%) if you invest at least $100,000. Schwab's S&P 500 Index fund and i-Shares S&P 500 Index ETF both charge just 9 basis points (0.09%). So it's difficult to understand why anyone would pay J.P. Morgan a fee for the privilege of investing in an S&P 500 Index fund with an expense ratio of 96 basis points (0.96%) since these funds are all identical.

But you can't feed an army of salesmen and women and turn a profit for shareholders on 9 or 10 basis points, which is why the brokerage firms' expense ratios are significantly higher and have a sales charge attached. The question is: why would you want to contribute to this?

The same caveat applies to exchange-traded funds or ETFs. Originally a small, rather stodgy variant on index mutual funds, ETFs have exploded in popularity and now come in a bewildering variety of shapes and flavors—worldwide there are now over 3,500 ETFs worth $1.4 trillion. The classic ETF was designed as a low-cost, plain vanilla, tax-efficient vehicle—much like an index mutual fund, except traded on the stock exchange so that you could buy or sell at any point in time, at a known price, rather than having to put in your order to buy a mutual fund at whatever its price was at the end of that day.

Among those 3,500+ ETFs there are many you should carefully avoid; however, if you stick with simple, low-cost, exchange-traded index funds these can be a useful complement to standard mutual funds. For example, if you wanted to invest in Vanguard's Dividend Appreciation Index fund in an IRA account at, say, Ameritrade, you couldn't buy the mutual fund, but for a small transaction fee could buy Vanguard's Dividend Appreciation ETF, which is invested in exactly the same way.

CONCLUSION

How passive should you be? That depends entirely on how much time and effort you want to dedicate to investing.

- If you've got better things to do with your time, you should just keep it simple by investing in total market index funds, both domestic and international (see the asset allocation section in chapter 12).

- If you want to be more active, you might consider tilting your allocation towards value indexes, or those indexes composed of dividend-payers, because history indicates these sectors have performed better than the market over time—although not in all periods.

• Even more active would be to analyze historical cycles of relative performance of large-cap vs. small-cap stocks, and value vs. growth stocks and to tilt in favor of whatever sector has most significantly *underperformed* in recent years, since in the stock market what has been last shall often be first and what has been first, last (see graphs below). However, this is a tricky game, and should only be played at the margins of your portfolio, with a small portion of your savings.

Exhibit 10
Relative Performance of U.S. Growth and Value Stocks
January 1, 1979 – June 30, 2013

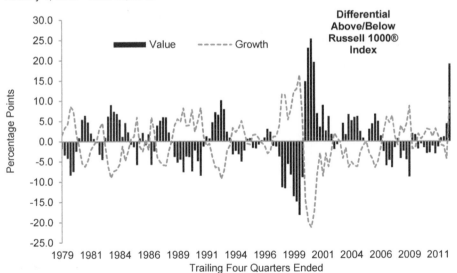

Exhibit 11
Relative Performance of U.S. Large- and Small-Cap Stocks
January 1, 1979 – June 30, 2013

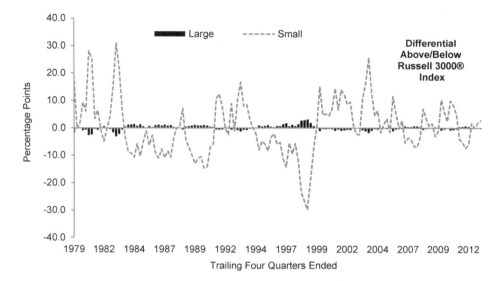

But note: although all these potential strategies involve active decisions, they do *not* require that you hire active managers—they should all be implemented through low-cost ETFs or index funds.

CHAPTER 11

Costs Matter Far More Than You Think

KINDS OF COSTS

Investors may pay four different kinds of costs:

1. Transparent costs, including:

- Mutual fund fees and expenses (which funds must clearly state in their materials).

- Fees for alternative investments, like hedge funds.

- Transaction costs for the purchase or sale of securities or ETFs. These are shown on your statement from the firm making the transaction for you.

- Wrap account fees.

2. Hidden costs, including:

- Bid-ask spreads on bonds.

- Costs buried in structured products.

- Increased trading costs incurred by mutual funds paying brokers so-called "soft dollars" for research.

- "Pay-to-play" monies paid by mutual funds to brokers who favor their products over those of rival firms ("payola for placement" as David Swensen puts it[lix]).

3. Tax costs.

- Under the current tax code, you pay 15% to 20% to the IRS every time you realize a long-term capital gain or earn a dividend in a taxable investment account.

- Since more than half the assets of mutual funds that invest in stocks are held in taxable accounts, you would think the managers of these funds would work extremely hard to minimize their investors' tax liabilities by minimizing turnover, harvesting losses to offset gains, and so on.

You would be wrong.

4. Opportunity costs.

• This is the difference between what you *could have* earned, if you had invested in X or Y, versus what you *actually* earned by investing in A or B.

• It may be the result of poor investment choices, or simply of paying higher fees and expenses than necessary and earning lower returns as a result.

TRANSPARENT COSTS

In 1971, John and Jane met at work and married at age 25. Like the rest of us, they didn't have any money to spare in the 1970s, but at the end of that decade they decided they really needed to start saving for their retirement.

• Helped by their company's matching program, each was able to save $1,000 every month in their 401(k)s, IRAs, and other accounts during the 1980s, $2,000 a month during the 1990s, and $3,000 in the last 10 years leading to their retirement at 65.

- So they each saved a total of $720,000 over 30 years.

- Jane invested in low-cost stock and bond market index funds with a combined expense ratio of 20 basis points (i.e., 0.2%).

- John thought he could do better with actively managed funds, which had a combined expense ratio of 120 basis points (i.e., 1.2%).

- Both maintained an allocation of 70% US equities, 30% US bonds, rebalanced annually.

- Miraculously, when they retired on December 31, 2010, at age 65 their portfolios had earned exactly the same average annual rate of return, before taking costs into account. (For the purpose of this illustration I'm ignoring the taxes they'd have paid on interest income, dividends and realized capital gains on the investments not held in tax-deferred accounts.)

Jane has, of course, avoided a risk that John took—the risk that active management would detract rather than add value over time. However, John was either lucky or reasonably skillful in his manager selection, since his account ended up earning the market rate of return (before expenses) over the 30 years he invested. However, John paid higher fees in pursuit of the higher returns that he did not, in fact, earn, so obviously Jane ended up with more money in her account.

How much more?

Well, based on the actual US stock and bond market returns over this 30-year period, on December 31, 2010 Jane's account would have been be worth $2,483,246 net of fees and John's $2,033,255. Yes, you read that right: John gave up almost $450,000 as a result of the higher fees he incurred.

You still think a percentage point here or there doesn't much matter?

- If they hadn't had to pay any fees at all, Jane and John would both have ended up with $2,586,372 (which illustrates the remarkable power of compounding over time when you consider that the money they invested over the years totaled only $720,000).

- Jane's cumulative total, after fees, is 4% less than this gross amount.

- John's cumulative total is 21% less.

- In other words, 17% of John's retirement kitty has evaporated without any commensurate gain in return.

If you think this illustration is unrealistic, you should go back and re-read the chapter on active management, and review the mountain of research referenced and quoted by all the authors I've cited. The evidence consistently shows that the odds were always stacked against John's finding active US equity and bond managers that would outperform the US stock and bond markets, net of costs, over any 30-year period.

In his *Winning the Loser's Game*, Charley Ellis cites a devastating analysis by Alliance Bernstein of the impact of various costs on an investor's cumulative wealth over a 35-year period from 1964 to 2000.

• The analysis assumes the investor begins with $3 million, invested equally in US stocks, bonds and T-bills.

• Before taxes, inflation and investment expenses, the stock portfolio would be worth $55 million by the end of 2000, the bond portfolio $15.5 million, and the T-bills $10.7 million.

• After taxes and inflation, not so great: stocks $5.4 million, bonds $1.2 million, and T-bills $800,000.

• Then deduct the average expenses you'd expect to pay if the money had been invested in mutual funds and the stocks end up with a real cumulative value of only $1.8 million, bonds $755,000 and T-bills $598,000.[lx]

MUTUAL FUND COSTS

As every student learns in Finance 101, the effect of compounding a small amount of money over a long period of time is very dramatic. This is why the higher costs incurred by John in the example above proves so damaging to his net worth by the time he retires.

In the highly efficient bond market, the scope for active managers to add value is minimal, which is why study after study has shown that the relative performance of bond funds is determined by their costs: the higher a fund's expense ratio, the worse its performance ranking.

In other words, it's very unlikely that the bond portion of John's portfolio would have added much value, even before taking costs into account.

On the stock side, if we assume that John's active fund charged 100 basis points (1%) more in fees and expenses than Jane's index fund did, then the manager of John's fund would have had to outperform the market index by 100 basis points (1%) on average, over time, just to keep up. This may not sound like much, but in fact it would put John's manager in quite elite company.

Because there is a massive industry promoting, advertising and selling actively-managed stock and bond funds carrying relatively high fees, it's not surprising that the industry continues to thrive despite destroying shareholder value.

What is astonishing, however, is that investors continue to buy "load" funds (i.e., those that charge a purchase commission) and funds that levy the notorious 12b-1 fee, which is an annual fee theoretically designed to enable fund management companies to recoup the cost of marketing their products and provide administrative services to clients.

In the real world, the performance of actively-managed stock funds that balloon in size almost always deteriorates. So why on earth should existing investors pay the fund to gather more assets? If they were asked to pay the fund to *stop* gathering additional assets by closing to new investors, that might make some sense, but in the perverse world of mutual fund sales, every fee makes sense.

In his *Common Sense on Mutual Funds*, Jack Bogle reports that by 2009, mutual fund companies were raking in $28 billion a year in 12b-1 fees from equity and bond funds. As Bogle comments, "This triumph of the interests of fund distributors over the interests of fund shareholders makes it clear whose interests come first in the mutual fund arena. (Hint: it isn't the fund shareholder.)"[lxi]

If you Google "mutual fund fees," you will find the SEC's "Mutual Fund Cost Calculator" pop up as an option. This will enable you to determine just how much bite from returns a specific amount of fees and expenses will take from an investment of $x that earns a return of y% over z years. The SEC also has a page listing all the various fees and expenses that may be charged by mutual funds, with good explanations of each.

Jack Bogle is the granddaddy of this subject. For decades he has documented and analyzed mutual fund expenses and hammered at the message that higher costs equate with lower returns.

Here is one example, assuming a nominal annual return of 10 percent on stocks. An equity mutual fund

*incurring annual expenses at the industry average
would lop off some two percentage points—fully one-
fifth of the market's annual return. Now, let's say that
inflation is 3 percent; then the market's real return is 7
percent, and costs would consume nearly one-third of
the market's reward. . . To state the obvious, the long-
term investor who pays least has the greatest opportunity to earn most of the real return provided by the
stock market.*[lxii]

Costs of Alternative Investment

For more exotic investments, like hedge funds or private
equity, the bar is set even higher, the costs even more daunt-
ing. There *are* some hedge funds whose returns justify their
fees—a very small percentage of the 9,000 total. The problem
is they're not open to individual investors like you and me
and require expert due diligence to identify. Nor can you rely
on a fund-of-funds manager to select winners for you; you'll
just end up with another layer of fees.

Individual investors should regard the $2 trillion hedge
fund industry, in aggregate, simply as a mechanism for transferring wealth from investors to fund managers.[lxiii] Stay
away.

The history of private market investment funds tells the
same story. Individual investors simply don't have access to
private equity or venture capital funds that generate net returns better than those of the public equity markets. Again,
high fees equate with low returns.

HIDDEN COSTS

The hidden costs incurred by many mutual funds do not show up on fund factsheets, although their existence may be acknowledged deep in the small print of a fund's prospectus. The trading costs of actively managed funds, for example, are not visible to investors, although their impact is detrimental to returns.[lxiv] As previously noted, "Hidden Causes of Poor Mutual-Fund Performance" in David Swensen's *Unconventional Success* gives a caustic and depressing account of the most egregious of such costs.

Beyond the mutual fund world, however, the two hidden costs investors are most likely to run into come when they buy and sell individual bond issues, and invest in structured products.

Cost of Bonds

When a brokerage firm sells to Joe Investor a bond it just bought from Mary Saver, Joe pays a significantly higher price than Mary received. How much higher depends on many factors, including the size of the transaction, but certainly enough to compensate the selling broker who gets a cut of the firm's profit on the transaction. This is the bid-ask spread.

Institutional buyers and sellers shop around for the best price, so in that world the spread is often wafer-thin. In the world of individual investors, who can't shop around for the best price and don't have access to Bloomberg terminals where they could determine what constitutes a fair price, it's generally wide enough to accommodate a good-sized truck.

You also probably lack the expertise to properly analyze a bond's credit risk and liquidity. For these reasons, you should not buy individual bonds unless you hire a fee-based investment advisor who has sufficient knowledge, scale, and experience to analyze the bond and access wholesale prices.

Cost of Structured Products

Structured products are packages of synthetic investment instruments specifically designed to appeal to needs that investors perceive are not being met by available securities. As a result, they are often packaged as asset-allocation tools to reduce portfolio risk. . . . These investments come with fancy names like Accumulators, Reverse Convertibles, STRATS, Super Track Notes, and a variety of forms of Principal Protection Notes.[lxv]

For example, an investment bank might offer you an investment paying x% in annual income, plus appreciation of principal linked to the performance of the stock market, but with protection against a decline in principal value greater than y%. When deconstructed (which takes some doing), such products always prove no more than expensive ways to achieve an outcome that could be realized more simply and cheaply through conventional asset allocations. It's all sizzle and very little steak.

Structured products are dressed up to sell and they succeed by appealing to investors' perpetual desire for reasonable returns with little risk. Financial advisors love them, for two reasons:

- First, when their clients are paralyzed with risk-aversion because of this or that financial crisis, it gives them a great story to sell—who doesn't want to earn a reasonable return with limited downside risk?

- Secondly, because such products pay handsome commissions.

To the financial advisor, it feels like a win-win: he or she earns a nice commission selling the product, and the clients are happy. It's very unlikely that the sales force has actually read the fine print and/or broken down the product into its component parts to understand exactly what they are selling. That's not their job. The issuer feeds them the sales pitch and they hit the phones.

But as author Larry Swedroe wisely advises,

[Investors] *should consider the transaction from the perspective of the issuer. The issuers of structured notes are generally large, sophisticated financial institutions who are not in the business of playing Santa Claus to investors. They don't issue securities with higher borrowing costs than they would otherwise have to pay. Investors need to ask themselves: Why do these firms issue these securities? The answer is obvious: The issuers have structured the securities to generate large profits for themselves, not for investors.*

If a security looks like it has a high yield or high return, then there is a high degree of risk involved. Even if you cannot see the risk, you can be sure it is there.[lxvi]

To illustrate (and hammer home the point!) here's a recent example, reported in *The New York Times* and several financial publications, including this from the *Financial Times* (2/6/2012):

The Asta/Mat funds are a textbook case: high-fee, highly leveraged strategies sold from 2002-2007 that it seems numerous advisers from Citigroup's former Smith Barney brokerage said their own company told them were relatively safe products that were designed to earn a slight premium over standard municipal bond holdings. . . these funds unraveled dramatically in early 2008 . . . eventually losing 71-97 per cent of their value and handing thousands of clients nearly $2bn in losses overall. . . . Similar products sold to US clients at rivals such as UBS Financial and Deutsche Bank also logged big losses.

Bottom line: keep away from structured products, including most annuity products, which are typically loaded with fees. If you're tempted by them because you don't know how to allocate your savings to earn a decent return without incurring a terrifying degree of risk, hire a qualified, fee-based investment advisor. In the long run, you'll sleep better, earn better returns, and avoid these hidden costs that can erode your returns like moths in your sweater drawer.

Cost of Wrap Accounts

As far back as the 1980s, recognizing that customers were increasingly concerned about the conflict-of-interest inherent in brokers being compensated on transactions, most brokerage firms created so-called "wrap" accounts which offered investors the option of paying a flat fee each year, computed as a percentage of total assets in their account. For the broker and the brokerage firm, this ensured a steady stream of income, as opposed to less predictable revenue on portfolio turnover.

When trading activity, commission income, margin account borrowing, and profits on bid-ask spreads all withered in the bear market of 2000-2003, the push to convert customers to flat fees accelerated dramatically.

If this fee arrangement sounds just like the fee-on-assets charged by independent investment advisory firms, that's not an accident. But it's not the same thing at all. You pay a registered investment advisor a fee to manage your money, with fiduciary responsibility for doing so in your best interests. Brokers provide advice and recommend products, but are not fiduciaries (although this may soon change).

Wrap-account fees run to somewhere between 1% and 2% of the assets in the account, which will often be invested in sub-optimal, in-house, actively managed mutual funds. If the same customer had been incurring annual commissions in excess of 1%, either he was a deluded stock jockey who thought he could outsmart the market by trading, or his account was being churned by an unethical salesman looking to maximize his commission income.

So for the broker and his employer, the flat fee is an excellent deal; for the customer, not so much. Better investment options are readily available elsewhere at far lower cost. For more detail on this topic, see Asher Hawkins' article, "Wrap Account Ripoff," of April 12, 2010, in Forbes.com. and "Flat Fees or Fat Fees? Did Your Client Get a Wrap Account or a Bum Wrap," by Douglas J. Schulz, at www.securitiesexpert.com.

TAXES

In some ways, the most shocking cost actively managed mutual funds inflict on their investors is taxes. Not because the funds levy taxes, but because they frequently ignore them. Yet each time a fund pays out realized capital gains, even if these are long-term gains, investors holding the fund in a taxable account net only 80 to 85 cents for every dollar paid out (unless they can shelter these gains by offsetting capital losses in other parts of their portfolios).

The key research on this topic is a 1993 article by Robert Jeffrey and Rob Arnott called, "Is Your Alpha Big Enough to Cover Its Taxes?" which concluded that active managers by no means generated sufficient excess returns (i.e., better-than-index returns) to come close to paying for investors' tax hit.[lxvii]

Author William Bernstein notes that the "typical large-cap fund distributes 5 to 10 percent of its value [in capital gains] in an average year," which knocks another 1% off investors' returns when federal and state taxes on such gains are taken into account.

When considering a mutual fund, investors often forget—or don't know—to ask about its accrued capital gains liability. "Liability" may seem like an odd term to use for something as beneficent as a capital gain, but it's eminently appropriate because if you buy a fund that has accrued capital gains that it might start distributing soon, you're on the hook for the taxes on those gains, even though you didn't own the fund during the period the gains were made.

The most painful example of this in recent memory occurred right after the dot.com bubble burst in 2000. David Swensen points out that not only did mutual fund companies and brokerage firms hawk technology funds right at the top of the bubble, only to see these crash and burn over the next three years, but the largest tech funds inflicted additional losses on their hapless clients by distributing over $3 billion in capital gains accrued during the run-up.

Because performance-chasing players bought high and sold low, an estimated 72 percent of contributed assets disappeared in the post-bubble break. Overly active fund

management exposed a further 24 percent of investor con-
tributions to potential tax liability."[lxviii]

But what can you do? Death and taxes are inevitable,
right? Yes, but minimizing the government's tax take is relatively simple.

• First, hold bond and REIT funds in a tax-deferred or tax-
exempt account, like an IRA.

• Second, invest in low-turnover stock index funds and
ETFs that don't distribute capital gains because they don't
realize them. Remember, index funds don't buy and sell in
an effort to add value; they simply hold every security in
the relevant index, and this lack of transactions means very
few realized gains and losses.

Readers interested in digging deeper into this topic
should first go to Bogle's *Common Sense on Mutual Funds*
whose chapter 13, "On Taxes," devotes 26 pages to the
subject.

OPPORTUNITY COSTS

Opportunity costs are both the simplest to describe and
the hardest to quantify. They are the costs investors incur by
making sub-optimal decisions that result in their having less

money at the end of the day than they would otherwise have had. The sources of such costs are myriad, but the most common are:

• Failing to allocate your financial assets according to a coherent investment plan that states clear investment objectives, time horizon, and risk tolerance. Too many investors, especially in defined-benefit pension plans, invest far too conservatively in "stable value" options that will not enable them to accumulate sufficient savings to fund their retirement. If you can't or won't develop a rational investment plan for yourself and your family, hire an investment advisor to do so for you.

• Failing to stay the course and follow the plan you or your advisor has laid out. Too many investors lack the basic knowledge of capital markets necessary to understand how to invest successfully and so they panic in bear markets and abandon their plan. Again, you should hire a qualified advisor if you lack such understanding and don't have the time or inclination to acquire it.

• Investing in higher-cost investment products and services. This would include paying fees and commissions to full-service brokers, mutual funds, and financial advisors for investment products that fail to deliver any value added. For example, a 2010 Morningstar article, "How Expense Ratios and Star Ratings Predict Success," concludes that "over every time period, the cheapest quintile funds in every asset class produced higher total returns than the most expensive quintile," and that expenses proved a better predictor of relative return among funds than did star ratings.[lxix]

• Failing to minimize unnecessary taxes on investment income and gains.

Any or all of these can seriously damage your investment results. For example, an analysis by the investment research firm Dalbar shows that the average US equity-fund investor earned 3.5% a year from 1992-2011 compared to an average annual return of 7.8% for the S&P 500 Index. Similar studies, covering various periods, have all reached this same conclusion.

How come? When you add up the fees paid to active managers that underperformed the market and the ruinous effects of lousy market timing decisions, you get from 7.8% to 3.5% pretty quickly.

Is this a big deal? Well, if you had invested $100 each month over this 20-year period, at an average annual return of 3.5% you'd end up with $34,576, whereas with a 7.8% average annual return, your total at the end of 2011 would be $55,956. That difference is enough to buy a small car.

CONCLUSION

Your investment objective should be to maximize your returns, within the risk parameters you've set, *net of all costs*. This means that high-cost products that generate exceptional after-cost returns are absolutely fine. Except that neither I nor any of the experts whose books and articles I've read know where you can find such products to invest in.

You can't invest cost-free, and you shouldn't attempt to avoid *all* taxes on your investments—if you try to do so, you'll end up with a sub-optimal asset allocation and incur significant opportunity costs. Nevertheless, every extra basis point you spend is likely to diminish your cumulative net worth, and so it's well worth your time to know what costs you're incurring and whether these are all necessary and worthwhile.

Part IV

CONSTRUCTING AND MANAGING AN INVESTMENT PORTFOLIO

CHAPTER 12

Writing Your Investment Plan and Diversifying Your Investments

Whether you go it alone or hire an investment advisor, you must develop a written *investment* plan that complements and completes your *financial* plan. If you don't, you'll be setting forth on an uncertain journey with no proper sense of direction and no road map on how to get wherever it is you're hoping to arrive. Once you have such a roadmap, and you *know* there will be hills and valleys ahead, it's much easier to stay on course so that you reach your intended destination.

Writing your plan needn't be an onerous process. In fact, here are some generic examples you could crib or adapt to your own circumstances. These are written in the third person for a reason: we're so emotional about our own money that it clarifies our thinking and keeps us on track if we pretend we're directing the investment portfolio of a third party. In other words, adopt (and describe) an investment persona, separate from yourself, and invest on his or her behalf.

SAMPLE INVESTMENT PLANNING DOCUMENT (I)

John and Patty Smith's Investment Plan, January 2, 2012
BACKGROUND

John Smith is 35 years old, Patty Smith is 34, and they have two children, Paul aged 4 and Mary, aged 1.

John is a patent attorney employed in the legal department of PRF Corporation. Patty is currently a stay-at-home Mom, but might return to full or part-time employment as a CPA when both children are of school age.

They have two financial goals:

First, to save enough to fund a significant percentage of their children's college education, from 2025 through 2032.

Secondly, to provide for their retirement, through 401(k) plan contributions, IRA accounts, and additional savings.

A separate document outlines John and Patty's financial plan, including how much they intend to save each year in each of these accounts as a means of achieving their financial objectives for both the college fund and the retirement fund.

This document complements that financial plan by outlining how their savings should be invested. Both plans will be reviewed annually, but changed only as, and when, there are material changes in John and Patty's circumstances.

The College Fund

1. The time horizon for the college fund is 14 years. That is, this money will be needed starting in year 14 and for seven years thereafter, assuming each child starts college at age 18 and graduates in four years.

2. The asset allocation for these funds should change as each child grows older. To this end, two college savings accounts will be set up and invested in Fidelity's 529 College Savings Plan Age-based portfolios. Paul's account will be invested in the 2024 portfolio and Mary's in the 2027 portfolio. Both will be invested in Fidelity index funds, the allocation among which will be adjusted by Fidelity as time passes.

The Retirement Fund

1. The time horizon for the retirement fund is 30 years plus.

2. Consequently, retirement savings should be invested 100% in stocks, now and for the next 20 years at least.

3. The volatility of global stock markets during this period is irrelevant and will generally be ignored.

4. Only if stock market valuations become dramatically extended, as a result of an extended bull market, should any savings be allocated to other asset classes.

5. If stock markets decline significantly and market valuations drop commensurately, John and Patty will try to accelerate their savings rate in order to take advantage of this opportunity.

*6. However, absent any such **extreme** conditions, they will simply keep adding to their portfolio through regular savings.*

7. This allocation will be implemented by investing 50% in the Schwab Total Stock Market Index Fund, 30% in the Schwab Fundamental International Large Company Index Fund, and 20% in the Vanguard Emerging Markets Index Fund.

*8. Since differences in performance among the funds will shift the totals away from the target percentages, at the start of each year John and Patty will **rebalance** their accounts, selling shares in the better-performing funds to buy more shares in the funds that have the worst returns, and/or by buying stock in the underweight fund with their additional savings until they arrive at the target percentages again.*

9. They will stick with this plan through thick and thin, strenuously resisting all impulses to second-guess the economy and the markets. They will alter this plan only if their personal financial circumstances materially change in unforeseen ways.

Sample Investment Planning Document (II)

Tom and Sarah Minter's Investment Plan,
September 30, 2011
BACKGROUND

Tom and Sarah Minter are both 58. They have two children, Lindsey, aged 32, and Sam, aged 30, who are both gainfully employed and financially independent.

Sarah is a senior project manager at a major accounting firm, and plans to retire at the end of 2014. Tom is chief financial officer of a regional wholesale grocery business. He plans to retire in five years.

Their house in the Chicago suburbs is paid for and they have a small mortgage on a condo in Sarasota, Florida, purchased in March 2008, where they spend some time each winter.

Neither of the companies they work for has a defined benefit plan, but both offer matching contributions to a 401(k) plan. For the past 15 years, Tom and Sarah have made the maximum possible contributions to both their 401(k) and their IRA accounts. In addition, they have managed to build up substantial additional savings in the past eight years.

However, they have earned no incremental return on their investment portfolio in the past 10 years, mostly as a result of the drop in the stock market, but also as result of what they perceive to have been poorly timed and inappropriate investment advice from the financial advisor with *whom they had invested their supplemental savings. They are looking for a sounder investment strategy.*

This experience, and their pending retirement, has led them to recognize that they need to develop a new financial and investment plan.

A financial planner has advised them that from the date of Tom's retirement, they could reasonably expect their projected savings of $1,700,000 to generate $8,250 each month over 30 years, at which time they would run out of money. However, he has warned them that a sharp decline in portfolio value in the early years of retirement would result in a materially lower monthly income.

Tom and Sarah also intend to sell the Chicago house and move full-time to Florida when he retires, and they believe this move will increase their retirement savings, giving them a reasonable cushion against outliving their money.

The Retirement Fund

1. *The time horizon for the retirement fund is 30 years plus.*

2. *But starting in year six, the Minters plan to rely on this fund for most of their living expenses.*

3. *These expenses should be expected to rise at least in line with consumer price inflation. Consequently, the retirement fund should still be invested primarily in stocks, now and for the next 15 years at least, since bonds yields are currently very low and bonds are vulnerable to rising inflation.*

4. However, stock market volatility could prevent the Minters from withdrawing enough money to sustain their standard of living. Consequently, they will invest 15% of their assets in intermediate Treasury bonds, 15% in high-quality municipal bonds, and 5% in TIPS. These will help them sustain spending in the event of a severe bear market in equities early in Tom's retirement years.

5. The remaining 65% will be invested in stocks, with an emphasis on high-quality companies with a history of rising dividend payments.

6. The portfolio will be rebalanced annually to maintain this allocation.

7. The allocation to stocks will only be reduced in the event of an extended bull market that leads to historically extreme valuations. Nor will the allocation to stocks be increased beyond 65% even if equity markets decline significantly. Absent any such extreme conditions, the Minters will simply keep adding to their portfolio through regular savings until Tom retires.

8. The policy allocation of 65% to stocks, 15% to Treasury bonds, 15% to municipal bonds and 5% to TIPS will be implemented as follows: 50% in the Vanguard Dividend Growth Fund, 20% in the Vanguard Total International Stock Index Fund, 15% in the Vanguard Long-Term Tax-Exempt Fund, 15% in the Vanguard Intermediate-Term

Treasury Fund, and 5% in Vanguard's Inflation Protected Securities Fund.

9. Since differences in performance among the funds will result in the actual allocations shifting away from these policy allocations, at the start of each year the Minters will **rebalance** their accounts, selling shares in the better-performing funds to buy more shares in the funds that have the worst returns, and/or by buying stock in the underweight fund with their additional savings until they arrive at the target percentages again.

10. They will stick with this plan through thick and thin, strenuously resisting all impulses to second-guess the economy and the markets.

11. When Tom retires, the Minters will review their financial plan and this asset allocation policy, to determine if it continues to meet their objectives.

COMMENT ON SAMPLE INVESTMENT PLANS AND ASSET ALLOCATIONS

The background statements here are not just added color for my readers' benefit—you should actually write out similar statements about yourself; stating who you are and what you are trying to achieve sets the stage.

Beyond that, these two investment plans are about as simple as I could make them. Many will argue that they are *too* simple, and much too heavily oriented to stocks.

On the first count—that these plans are too simple and depend too heavily on stocks and bonds:

• I would endorse the idea of adding, say, Real Estate Investment Trusts (REITs) and natural resource funds to these allocations. The source of money for such allocations should be the stock market portion.

• As always, investors should seek out low-cost funds for these allocations. For example, Vanguard has a REIT index fund and an excellent, low-cost, actively managed Energy Fund.

• Such an allocation to a mix of REITs and natural resource funds should be enough to make a difference in the total portfolio. For example, the Minters might consider taking 15 percentage points from their allocation to stocks and investing in REIT and natural resource funds amounting to 15% of their total portfolio.

• I would only caution that REIT funds are quite volatile, with valuations swinging cyclically from significantly overvalued to significantly undervalued.[lxx] So I would encourage anyone selecting a REIT fund to to wait for an undervalued period. Also be aware that REITs pay out most of their income as *unqualified* dividends that are taxed at

204 / Simple Smart Investing

ordinary income tax rates, so they are not tax-efficient investments and should be held in an IRA or other tax-advantaged account.

• As for natural resource funds: although such funds will tend to track the broader stock market, they should outperform during periods of sharply rising inflation, which may cause other equities to sell off.

On the second count—that these plans are too heavily oriented to stocks—I have two defenses:

• First, capital markets history shows us that the longer the time horizon, the greater the probability that stocks will outperform bonds by a wide margin. Moreover, when one takes inflation into account, bonds have generated negative real returns far more often than stocks, even over long periods. As I've said repeatedly, we shouldn't assume the future will mirror the past; nevertheless, the fundamental reasons for these two facts haven't changed.

• My second defense is that even for periods as long as 25 years or more, how much you are likely to earn in any asset class is crucially dependent on your starting point.

• Today, bond yields are extremely low, after the longest and best bull run in bond market history over the past 25 years.

• This means that bond valuations are high and bond returns very vulnerable to rising inflation and rising interest rates.

• In contrast, over the past 12 years stock markets have experienced one of the worst bear markets in history and are selling now at more reasonable (although not cheap) valuations.

No one can predict where the stock market might go over the next year or two (see chapter 4 on forecasting). It might well suffer another sell-off. Nobody knows. But for truly long-term investors, this is not a bad time to invest in stocks. Yes, the news seems pretty bad, pessimism rife, governments inept, voters angry and demoralized. Maybe the market has not yet fully discounted the storms that could blow in from Europe, from China, from the Mid-East. We don't know. But these are exactly the sort of conditions the great investors like Warren Buffett relish. They buy when others are fearful and sell when others are greedy and gloating. You should, too.

The markets offer no guarantees. Especially stock markets. All we have to go on is historical precedent and some faith that across its many variations around the globe, capitalism will continue to reward those who risk their capital in equity investments. Not every equity investor and not in all periods, but in the aggregate and over the long term.

Note that the Smiths and the Minters have pretty secure jobs that seem relatively well insulated from financial crises.

This should allow them to take more investment risk than couples more vulnerable to the economic cycle. For example, a 35-year old investment banker should take less investment risk with his savings than a 35-year old orthopedic surgeon because the banker's income is at far greater risk in a slump.

WHY OWN BONDS?

Bonds are far less volatile than equities, so bond investors have far greater assurance that their money will be there, more or less intact, when they need it. But risk and return are two sides of the same coin: historically, bond investors have paid for this greater stability with substantially lower returns, both over the long term (e.g., since 1900) and over most interim periods. Except for TIPS (Treasury Inflation-Protected Securities), which yield almost nothing today, bond income is eroded daily by inflation, whereas stock market dividends have risen steadily over time, maintaining their purchasing power. So, why own bonds?

If you have enough money, and investment experience, perhaps you don't need to own bonds at all. For example, if you're a retiree with $5 million to invest and can live on a pre-tax income of $200,000, you could construct a portfolio of low-cost stock index funds that would yield 4% in dividends. The market goes up, the market goes down—so what? As long as the vast majority of companies keep paying those dividends, which over time should at least keep pace with inflation, the ups and downs of the stock market shouldn't concern you.

That's why I added the proviso that you need "investment experience" to invest like this—only the most experienced (and/or knowledgeable) investor can sail through a storm like 2008-09 without panic.

Of course, you'd also have to get through occasional periods when even relatively strong companies are forced to reduce their dividends. For example, after the brutal 2008-09 financial crisis, large dividend-paying US companies cut their dividends about 30%, and their counterparts in overseas developed markets by more than 60%.

So the argument for bonds—Treasury bonds—is that they've provided a safe haven when storms have buffeted the equity markets. Here's the evidence:

Exhibit 12
How Have U.S. Bonds Performed When the U.S. Stock Market Has Dropped Sharply?
Largest Stock Market Declines 1926–2012

Stock Market Peak	Stock Market Trough	S&P 500 Index	U.S. 10-Yr Treasuries	High-Quality Corporate Bonds
8/31/1929	6/30/1932	-86.0	9.8	6.9
2/28/1937	3/31/1938	-53.0	1.4	2.9
10/31/2007	2/28/2009	-52.6	18.2	-3.5
12/31/1972	9/30/1974	-46.2	1.6	-10.3
3/31/2000	9/30/2002	-45.6	37.0	38.8
10/31/1938	4/30/1942	-41.8	14.1	14.6
11/30/1968	6/30/1970	-32.9	-2.9	-7.6
8/31/1932	2/28/1933	-32.6	2.9	5.6
8/31/1987	11/30/1987	-30.2	2.4	1.9
5/31/1946	6/30/1949	-26.2	4.4	5.8
1/31/1934	3/31/1935	-24.2	10.0	15.4
6/30/1933	10/31/1933	-18.0	1.0	2.7
	Average		8.3	6.1
	Max		37.0	38.8
	Min		-2.9	-10.3

Notwithstanding current concerns over government indebtedness, Treasury bonds are still regarded as effectively free of credit risk. That's important. When recessions or financial crises hit and interest rates drop, corporate bonds (encumbered with credit risk) do not behave like Treasury bonds. Instead of appreciating, they may decline in value because investors are afraid the companies may have trouble meeting their debt-service payments. Mortgage-backed securities are vulnerable to pre-payment during these periods, also making them less secure investments than Treasuries.

CONCLUSION

Your investment plan should be integrated with your financial plan.

• It should be written out so that you can refer to it in times of stress.

• How you allocate your savings across different investment options should reflect your age, time horizon, and objectives.

• Having mapped out your intended course, you must commit to following that plan.

• This includes regular savings and regular rebalancing to bring your actual asset allocation back in line with what's mapped out in your plan. If you can automate both, so much the better.

• You should review your plan once a year, however briefly, *not* in light of current market conditions, which you should largely ignore, but in light of your own circumstances. If those have not changed materially, for better or worse, there should be no logical reason to change course.

• You should implement your asset allocation by investing in low-cost index funds and ETFs.[lxxi]

• REITs and Taxable bonds (i.e., Treasury bonds and TIPS) should be held in tax-advantaged accounts.

CHAPTER 13

Understanding and Managing Investment Risk

Investors are in the business of deploying capital in hopes of earning a return. Always and everywhere, since the beginning of human enterprise, this has entailed risk of loss.

- You lend money, but the borrower can't pay it back.

- You buy shares in a promising company, but it goes bust.

- You tuck money under the mattress, but inflation erodes its value like rats gnawing on cheese.

So risk management lies at the very heart of investing and there's no such thing as a "risk-free" investment. But the two golden rules of risk management are:

1. Never incur a risk you're not likely to get paid for.

2. Never make an investment where the risk is great but the prospective return is small. On the contrary,

investors should seek opportunities where the risk: return ratio is skewed in their favor, rather than against them.

The purpose of risk management is to clearly define just what risks one can try to reduce, and why, and over what time horizon, and at what potential cost.

What risks must investors run in pursuit of return and what risks can they avoid?

And what can they do to reduce or manage the risks they must incur?

BEHAVIORAL RISKS

This is the first and most important risk category you face because if you can't manage it, you'll fail as an investor no matter what else you do.

Like all decisions that require our peering into the uncertain future, investment decisions are always based on incomplete information. Nevertheless, given such information as we have, those decisions should be made on the basis of logical, objective, knowledgeable analysis of the facts on hand.

But they aren't. Instead, we infect them with our personal biases, "gut instincts," irrelevant assumptions, and a veritable Pandora's box-load of all-too-human irrational propensities. Although we can't hope to eliminate these infections, we can and should diagnose and contain them.

The most common mistake we make is to overrate the importance of recent results and extrapolate short-term trends into the uncertain future. This is particularly dangerous during periods of market euphoria, like the dot.com boom of the late 1990s, or extreme despair, like that of late 2008 to early 2009, when the whole financial edifice seemed to be collapsing.

The financial media outlets frantically spray gasoline on these fires, since for them booms and crises are manna from heaven, bringing more viewers, more readers, more subscribers looking for advice and direction. As a result, the daily barrage of noise that blankets the investment world at the best of times becomes a constant screech that can easily overwhelm us and lead us to bad decisions.

When markets are falling, we instinctively feel that risk is rising, and when markets are rising, that risk is ebbing. In the short term, this may be spot on since markets do often run on momentum over short periods.

For long-term investors this instinct is dead wrong. So if you're investing long-term, for your retirement or for your infant son's college education, you need to know how and why it's wrong.

Understanding long-term market cycles is your best defense against panic. As legendary investor John Templeton famously remarked, the most dangerous words in the investment lexicon are "this time it's different."

Without some knowledge of capital markets history, you're likely to fall into the human tendency to overweight the most recent news, and focus on evidence that supports your reactions, ignoring or downplaying contrary evidence.

So go back and read chapter 3 again!

Behavioral Responses to Trauma

What happens when we humans (and, indeed, other animals) are slammed by shock? Unless trained otherwise, our instincts tell us to retreat, conserve, seek the comparative safety of groups, and search for a path out of danger. These are ancient survival instincts, hard-wired.

Slammed by *financial* shock, the same instincts lead us to:

• A dramatic rise in our aversion to perceived risk (gimme cash!).

• An overwhelming impulse to flee.

• A dramatic shrinking of our normal investment time horizon—the fact that we won't need to tap this money for another 20 years suddenly seems irrelevant.

• A tendency to extrapolate current trends all the way to Armageddon.

• A deep desire to latch on to anyone who seems able to explain what is going on and what will happen next—and so alleviate the misery of our deep uncertainty.

Under such conditions, we often make mistakes that cost us dearly: long-term plans are abandoned and rational investment policies discarded.

So the question is: can we train ourselves in some way to override these natural instincts?

Countering Behavioral Risk

During a financial crisis, like that of 2008-09, older investors are generally better than younger ones at managing their instinct to panic with the stampeding herd. This is because older investors may have seen this sort of thing before and know that it's not, in fact, the end of the world. So some experience as well as knowledge of capital markets history is an invaluable antidote to instinctive panic.

The chart below should help mitigate the fear that grips our guts when markets crash.

Exhibit 13
U.S. Stock Market Rolling Ten-Year Real Returns (i.e., after inflation)
January 31, 1869 – June 30, 2013

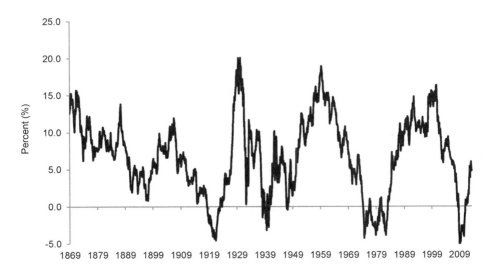

Notice that the data comprising this chart goes back 150 years. The lines are drawn by connecting data points that represent the previous 10-year's return for the US stock market. For long-term investors, two rather obvious points are worth stressing.

First obvious point:

• In complete contrast to what most investors felt at the time, March 2009 was a great time to invest in US stocks. The preceding 10-year real (i.e., inflation-adjusted) rate of return was the worst on record, with an average annual real rate of return of -5.9%. No wonder we all felt so bad!

• But as the chart below makes abundantly clear, if you invest at the end of a really bad decade, your chances of earning outsized returns over the subsequent decade are very good indeed.

• In fact, historical data show that on average investors in US stocks earned 14.8% per year, after inflation, in those decades that followed the 25 worst 10-year periods for the stock market.

• The lowest real rate of return for any decade following one of those bad 10-year periods was 6.8%, which is still a better return than the long-run stock market average.

Exhibit 14
U.S. Stock Market Returns Are Cyclical
The worst ten-year periods on record, and subsequent ten-year returns

Ten-Year Period Ending	Worst Trailing Real Return (%)	Subsequent Real Return (%)
02/28/2009	-5.9	---
03/31/2009	-5.4	---
01/31/2009	-5.1	---
04/30/2009	-4.9	---
06/30/2009	-4.7	---
06/30/1921	-4.6	16.2
12/31/1920	-4.4	16.3
09/30/1974	-4.3	7.3
07/31/1921	-4.2	15.1
11/30/1920	-4.2	16.6
05/31/2009	-4.2	---
08/31/2010	-4.1	---
05/31/1920	-4.1	20.3
01/31/1921	-4.0	16.3
03/31/1921	-4.0	16.9
08/31/1921	-3.9	15.4
02/28/1921	-3.9	17.4
07/31/1982	-3.9	14.8
11/30/1978	-3.9	9.7
06/30/2010	-3.9	---
06/30/1920	-3.8	18.5
12/31/2008	-3.8	---
12/31/1974	-3.8	6.8
05/31/1921	-3.7	13.8
07/31/2009	-3.7	---
	Average	14.8
	Max	20.3
	Min	6.8
	% Positive	100.0

Second obvious point:

• Stock market returns are not linear, they are cyclical: what goes up comes back down and what comes down goes back up.

• Many seasoned investors believe that stock markets are mean reverting (i.e., they return to their average level). But actually this is wrong: markets shift from high to low, passing through the average en route; then they reverse, moving from low to high. The average is just a milepost along the way.

• Although nobody rings a bell at the top or a gong at the bottom, a chart like that in Exhibit 14 can at least indicate when the stock market has reached, or perhaps passed, relatively extreme points in the likely distribution of returns.

• We should respond by ignoring our instinctive euphoria or despair and rebalancing religiously to make sure we're not in fact allowing our investment portfolio to become more or less exposed to stock market risk than we have planned.

Other Behavioral Risks

There are many other behavioral risks lying in wait for unwary investors. Perhaps the most potent, other than those outlined above, is over-confidence, which we exacerbate by remembering our successes far more than we do our failures. Both traits have evolutionary advantages for homo sapiens, but for investors, not so much. The best antidote is careful measurement and record keeping of results, which is why I've devoted an entire chapter to how you should keep track of your investment performance.

Finally, we should recognize that we're all suckers for a good story. If you're a geeky quant, you're probably constantly frustrated by your fellow humans' feeble attention span for data and numbers. Every good salesman knows this cold. Although I can muster decades of robust data demonstrating the idiocy of investing in the newly issued stock of small growth companies, I don't stand a chance against a good salesman with a sizzling story:

- "I don't know if I can get you an allocation, but I gotta tell you, our analysts think this one's the next Google."

- "With the rapid growth of the consumer class in China, our guys in Asia see this as a slam dunk."

- "Gene-therapy is the most promising breakthrough in cancer treatment in decades and this company's right on the cutting edge."

You feel the buzz, huh? The chance to get in on the ground floor? The lure of the big score? The opportunity to be a player with the big boys?

Almost irresistible. Believe me: learn to resist.

INFLATION RISK

Virtually all investment results are reported in nominal terms; that is, without any adjustment for inflation. This is understandable—after all, that's how we count our money—but inadequate, because we also need to know whether a dollar tomorrow will buy more or less than it did yesterday. Almost certainly the answer is "less"; for example, $100 in January 1980 was worth only $34 by July 31, 2011.

If we simply ignore inflation risk in our evaluation of investment options, we run the danger of making bad choices.

For example, studies have shown that far too many participants in 401(k) plans allocate far too much money to so-called "stable value" options, such as money-market and short-term bond funds that are unlikely to earn any return at all after inflation.

Now, as long as your paycheck outpaces inflation and promotions move you up the salary scale, a modest rise in the CPI shouldn't bother you, since your own purchasing power will be rising faster. But what about the purchasing power of your savings? At a minimum, those also need to keep pace with inflation, and preferably earn some incremental real rate of return. Even in retirement you can't afford to see your purchasing power erode.

This is why I emphasize investing in stocks not only for long-term savings plans, but also for retirees. Equity investments are a claim on real assets, and although an unexpected spike in the rate of inflation will precipitate a bear market, as it did in the 1970s, over the long term stocks will almost certainly generate positive returns after inflation, as corporate earnings and dividends rise.

What about inflation-linked bonds? Many advisors recommend significant allocations to Treasury Inflation Protected Securities (TIPS) in retirement savings accounts. I'm not so sure a large allocation to TIPS is such a good idea. Of course, if you buy-and-hold TIPS when they are issued and hold them until they mature, they will provide protection against consumer price inflation. But how much you'll actually earn is, of course, a function of how much interest they pay.

Because TIPS are designed as an inflation hedge, it's usually their real rate of interest that's quoted (i.e., the inflation-adjusted rate). That has recently been negative, and today (June 2013) has only just crawled into positive territory.

The interest rate TIPS pay has tracked the nominal (i.e., pre-inflation) rate paid by conventional Treasury bonds, which means that we should expect their real interest rates to rise when the Federal Reserve allows rates in general to rise. When that happens, the price of TIPS issued today will go down along with regular Treasury bonds. With TIPS, rising inflation may offset the decline, but it's impossible to predict when and by how much.

Thus, if you buy into a fund that invests in inflation-indexed bonds, you should not assume that it will necessarily appreciate exactly in line with inflation. Rising inflation will indeed push up the price of the fund's holdings, but rising interest rates might offset some or all of that increase.

All that said, over the long term, inflation will be the most important factor, and so I agree that some allocation to TIPS is a good inflation hedge in retirement savings with a time horizon of 20 years or so.

But if the real interest rate paid by TIPS were to increase over time to about 2.5% or more, then I would become much more enthusiastic about larger allocations in your portfolio.

However, risk management is a game of whack-a-mole: as soon as you bang down one risk, you cause another to pop right up. So when you squash inflation risk by investing in stocks, whoosh! up pops stock market risk, which manifests itself in stock market volatility.

STOCK MARKET VOLATILITY

As the chapter on capital markets history showed, virtually all investors with 10 years or longer to invest should generally put most of their money in stocks, since these offer the best long-term defense against inflation and over time are likely to provide significantly higher real returns than bonds.

But there is no return without risk and the risk inherent in stocks is volatility. This means that the value of your stock market investments could suddenly decline significantly, no matter how long you hold them.

Why Does Volatility Matter?

Volatility matters because it creates the risk that you won't have money when you need it.

For example, Susan has read that over the long term the average annual return of the US stock market has been slightly more than 6.0% after inflation and that this seems as good an assumption as any other for estimating future returns. So over the years she invests her savings entirely in stocks, with the aim of having $2,000,000 when she reaches retirement age, so that she can subsequently withdraw $120,000 each year (i.e., 6%) to live off. After all, if stocks return 6% annually, after inflation, and she takes out 6% each year, then her $2,000,000 retirement fund should remain intact, providing spending money for as long as she lives. Right?

Wrong.

Here's where her logic has gone awry:

• Sure enough, Susan reaches her goal of $2,000,000 just as she retires on December 31.

• She lives off her last paycheck and year-end bonus until March 31 of the following year, then withdraws $120,000 for the next 12 months' spending, as planned. So far so good.

• The stock market hasn't gone anywhere during the first quarter, so after that withdrawal her fund is now worth $1,880,000.

• But during the next 12 months stocks plummet, down 40%, so now her portfolio value is only $1,128,000.

• As an experienced investor, Susan knows not to panic—she's seen markets behave this way before, and they've always recovered.

• What she hasn't thought through is that if she now takes out her annual $120,000, it will represent over 10% of her fund's new asset value, not 6%, as planned, leaving her with only $1,008,000.

• So even if she were to take no more withdrawals after that, her portfolio would now have to almost double in value to get back to $2,000,000.

• That might happen over a period of several years, but not if she continues to withdraw $120,000 each year.

• In other words, if she keeps tapping water from the barrel at that rate, she'll drain it dry pretty soon even if there's a decent flow coming in the top.

Susan's assumption of a 6% average annual real rate of return for stocks isn't to blame here; what she forgot is that an average of anything is only half the story; the other half is the range. If you know that the *average* height of American men is 5'9" should you be surprised to meet someone who's 6'4"?

No. Because the average doesn't tell you what any specific man's height might be.

Similarly, the long-term *average* annual real rate of return of 6% for stocks doesn't tell us anything about how much stocks might return in any given one-, three-, five-, 10- or even 25-year period. If your time horizon is infinite and you don't plan to withdraw money to fund your spending needs, that's one thing, but not many of us are in that position. We plan to live off of our retirement savings. So we'd better understand the risks associated with stock market volatility if we invest in stocks.

Susan needed a more balanced portfolio, including some Treasury and municipal bonds that would appreciate in value when the economic weakness that caused the stock market to sell off also resulted in declining interest rates. She could then draw her living expenses from her bond portfolio while also rebalancing her asset allocation by shifting money from bonds into stocks, so that when the market recovered she would reap the benefit.

It's perhaps worth noting, as an aside, that Susan couldn't just take her $2,000,000 when she retired and stick it in a safe bank account, money market fund, or Treasury bills.

- First, this would generate taxable income, reducing the net amount available to her.

- Secondly, if she withdrew $120,000 each year, she would run out of money in about 17 years.

• Third, she would be exposing her savings to the danger of higher inflation that could significantly reduce her purchasing power during her retirement years.

So she does need to remain invested—just not invested 100% in stocks.

How Volatile are Equities?

For those of a mathematical bent, volatility is measured by the standard deviation of returns. For example, the real average annual return of US stocks since 1900 has been 6.1%, with a standard deviation of 18, which means that two-thirds of these one-year returns fell between 24.1% and -11.9%.

As the time horizon lengthens, volatility declines: the standard deviation of five-year real returns has been 8.8, of 10-year real returns 5.8, and of 25-year real returns 2.4. There's absolutely no way to predict future volatility, but no good reason to think it might change, so most market analysts just assume it will be like that of the past.

The key question: Outside that two-thirds range, what's the maximum downside?

The graph below shows the *distribution* of average annual nominal and real returns for US equities over different time periods from 1900-2010.

Exhibit 15
Range of Historical U.S. Stock Market Returns for Different Time Periods
1900–2012

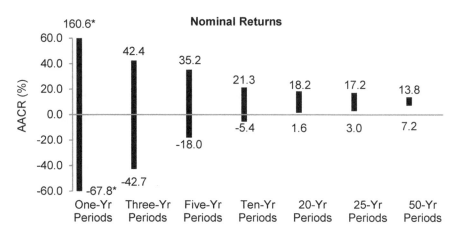

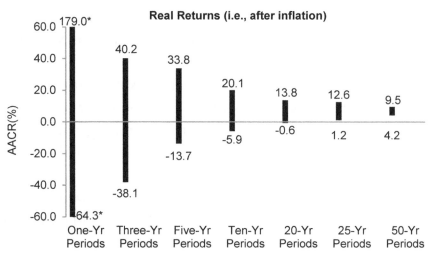

* Graph capped for scale purposes

What's striking here is how divergent returns have been even over periods as long as 25 years.

• Although the *average* annual real return for every 25-year period since 1900 is 6.7%, the distribution around that average is from 1.2% to 12.6%.

• This makes for a huge difference in terminal wealth: for example, $100,000 invested in a tax-free account that earned that annual 12.6% real return over 25 years would be worth $1,942,942 even after adjusting for inflation.

• On the other hand, $100,000 earning just 1.2% annually over 25 years would have a real terminal value of only $134,745. Wow! What a difference!

Managing Volatility Risk and Retirement Spending

Although you can't control stock market returns, you can arrive at a reasonable guesstimate—for periods of 10 years or longer—of whether they're likely to fall in the top, middle or bottom of their range (see the section on stock market valuations in chapter 3, "The Capital Markets"). You can also control how exposed you are to stock market volatility.

Because volatility is far higher for shorter than for longer time periods, the amount of volatility you can tolerate is a function of your investment time horizon and the amount you plan to withdraw from your investment portfolio. In the example above, Susan's mistake was to assume that she could readily withdraw $120,000 each year because that represented 6% of her portfolio's value at retirement, and it seemed reasonable to assume stocks would continue to generate real returns averaging about 6% over the long term.

In the first place, 6% is too high a percentage; most advisors recommend a rate of 4% or less if you want to ensure that you don't run out of money before you die.[lxxii] But Susan had focused not on the percentage, but on the dollar amount, and if you do that, you'd better ensure that this amount will not exceed, say, 6% of the portfolio's value even at the trough of a vicious bear market.

So there's no one answer for how much volatility is tolerable: this depends on how much money you have relative to how much you plan to withdraw over what time period. For example, if you have a large enough portfolio that you can comfortably live off the dividends generated by your stocks, the volatility of the stock market should be of little concern—it's the volatility of the dividend stream that matters to you, and historically that's been relatively stable over time.

Most of us don't have that much money, however, so we can't afford to be 100% invested in stocks as we approach retirement and the need to start living off our savings. We don't care about upside volatility at all—the more upside the better!—so the question is how to protect our nest egg against those periodic downdrafts in the stock market.

The obvious way is to have less and less money in stocks as you approach retirement. Or in the case of saving for your child's college education, as the time horizon narrows from 20 years to 10 and then five, you should steadily shift virtually all the money into fixed income investments maturing on the dates you'll need to pay those tuition bills.

The problem with shifting to bonds as you approach retirement is that a relatively affluent and healthy 65-year-old can reasonably hope to live for another 20 years, and must plan for his savings to last at least another 35 years, just in case. Anyone with a 30-year horizon should have a significant allocation to stocks to protect against inflation.

For retirees, stock market volatility is a problem if it affects their spending. If you plan to spend a fixed amount, as Susan did, you run the risk of spending too high a percentage of your assets and depleting them before you die. If you plan to spend a fixed percentage of your assets—for example, 5%—then the actual amount of money this represents may vary considerably from year to year.

The solution is to maintain a relatively high exposure to stocks (i.e., 60% to 65%), with the rest split evenly between tax-free bonds and a spending reserve consisting exclusively of Treasury notes with maturities from two to 10 years—no corporate bonds, no mortgage-backed securities, just Treasuries.

- In the normal course of events, your spending will come from muni-bond interest, stock dividends, and perhaps from some sale of your stock market investments.

- But it should never exceed 5% of the average value of your assets over the past three years.

- If markets go on a tear, you should not allow the dollar amount of your withdrawals to increase much more than the rate of inflation from year to year, but should park any "excess" in a spending reserve (aka rainy day) fund consisting of more US Treasuries.

• When weak economic activity triggers a decline in the stock market, interest rates will decline and your Treasuries will appreciate.

• You can now tap this part of your portfolio to sustain spending while stocks are in the doldrums.

The idea here is that you never want to sell stocks to support your spending needs when the stock market is depressed. Stocks are the growth engine of your portfolio, and if you sell them when they're down, you're eating your seed corn.

AVOIDABLE RISKS

Active Risk

You incur active risk when you invest in an actively managed fund, or hire an investment manager who picks stocks or bonds or funds on your behalf. It's a risk, because if your savings plan is predicated on your earning the return of the stock market, but your actively managed funds or accounts underperform the stock market by, say, one percentage point a year over 20 or 30 years, you'll end up with a lot less money than if you had invested in a passive index fund instead.

Obviously, the only reason to assume this kind of risk is because you think you'll earn more than the market return, not less. Of course all active managers on the planet are convinced they'll do just that. But is such optimism justified? Is this a risk worth taking? As the chapter on Active Management explains, the odds are heavily stacked against you.

In short, most investors should avoid active risk in most of their portfolio because they are unlikely to get paid for it and risk earning less than they otherwise would.

Leverage

Investors leverage their portfolios when they borrow money to increase their stock holdings. They do this in the hope that they'll earn more from their investments than the cost of the debt they incur, and thereby enhance their total return. As the chief investment officer of Princeton's endowment fund once said to me, "Leverage is the crack cocaine of investing. It feels so good when you do it, you just want to do more."

But like crack, leverage is a terrible addiction that destroys lives. The sickening acceleration of downward momentum that always occurs in bear markets is caused by leveraged investors desperately scrambling to liquidate their holdings in order to meet margin calls.

- When you invest borrowed money, the lender demands collateral in the form of your financial assets.

• As the value of those assets declines in a bear market, the lender demands that you put up more cash (or securities) to compensate for the lower value of the collateral.

• But most leveraged investors can only raise the necessary cash by selling assets, which further depresses their price . . . which means they have to raise more cash . . . which means they have to sell more assets . . .which means . . .

And so it goes, all the way to bankruptcy.

The old saying tells us that a fool and his money are soon parted. In the investment world, leverage is probably the quickest way to achieve this outcome.

In a word: Don't.

Chasing Yield (especially structured products)

"Anyone peddling promises of higher yield without higher risk is either a liar or a fool. . . Any time anyone tries to sell you any investment on premises like these put one hand on your wallet and run for your life; you are about to be snookered." So writes Jason Zweig in his chapter, "Finding your Fixed Income" in *The Little Book of Safe Money* (pages 53-66). Anyone tempted to invest in a fund with a benign name like Yield Plus, Enhanced Cash, or Short-Term Global Income, which promises higher returns with less risk should read this salutary chapter, where Jason documents the savage losses investors have incurred in such funds over the years.

The bottom line is crystal clear: the higher the yield of a given investment, the greater the risk of loss of some sort. This might be a risk as benign as slower growth from higher-yielding stocks, like those of utility companies. But it might also be risk of default of a high-yielding corporate bond (e.g., Lehman Brothers) or the collapse of a structured product.

Two circumstances have made yield-chasing a more common, and malign, kind of risk than in the past.

• The first: as more and more boomers retire, the financial services industry has become increasing creative in constructing products that appear to offer attractive income at low risk.

• The second: current interest rates are so low that retiree standbys like CDs, money-market funds, and Treasury bills generate almost no income.

• This makes yield-hungry investors vulnerable to sales pitches for well-packaged structured products from investment banks, brokerage firms, and insurance companies.

• These take many forms, but typically involve offering investors a fixed yield (e.g., 4%), plus any increase in the price of the S&P 500, with some downside protection against loss in exchange for limited liquidity (e.g., you can only redeem your investment at the end of each quarter).

Sounds pretty good, right? Not when you read the fine print, reams of which can be found in the prospectus, couched in almost impenetrable prose. That's where the devil is hiding—in those details.

Cambridge Associates regularly receives requests from its private clients to deconstruct structured products pitched to them by investment banks. Suffice it to say that these are generally high-priced roach motels, conveying far more risk, far higher hidden costs, far less prospective return, and far less liquidity than at first appears.

Don't be naïve. Even the wizards of Wall Street can't conjure returns out of thin air. They have to be generated somehow, somewhere from the underlying returns of the capital markets. So if you're offered a product that seems to offer an unusually high yield or return, with a promise of limited downside risk, don't be a sap. The risks are there, even if you can't spot them. The high fees are there, even if they aren't apparent. It's all in the prospectus, if you can hire a lawyer, a CPA and investment expert to pick through the details. Stay away.

In short, you never get something for nothing, so don't delude yourself into thinking that you can earn a higher yield without incurring some offsetting cost or risk. This is not to say you should avoid higher yielding stocks—not at all—only that you should recognize that the quid pro quo is likely to be slower dividend growth.

So, don't chase yield and stay well away from all structured products.

CONCLUSION

One of the first things any financial planner or investment advisor will try to learn from a new client is his or her risk tolerance. But we don't have a set risk tolerance—our tolerance for investment risk shifts all over the place, almost day to day, depending on the weather, our children's behavior, today's news, and of course how our investment portfolio has been doing recently.

If we don't recognize and acknowledge that soaring or plummeting markets will trigger instinctual, emotional reactions that might well result in our making bad decisions, we're kidding ourselves. Knowing that we'll be tempted to ditch our carefully laid plans and pull the plug at just the wrong time when markets crash, we need to arm ourselves in advance with some historical data that will remind us that this is how markets behave, and that the time to wade deeper into the water is when everyone else is scrambling to get out after the wave has already hit them.

Inflation and volatility are the two other risks investors must manage. Because money is only worth what it will buy, now and in the future, we should focus more on inflation-adjusted than on nominal dollar returns. This means that long-term investors should have most of their money in stocks rather than in bonds, since stocks are claims on real assets and bonds (except for inflation-linked bonds) are claims on nominal cash payments whose value is steadily eroded by inflation.

But stock market volatility is dangerous for anyone whose

objective is to save for a specific purchase, on a date certain—college tuition, for example, or that vacation cottage in Maine. If you know exactly when you'll need the money, you should move steadily from stocks into short- to intermediate-term bonds as the date approaches, with virtually 100% invested in bonds and cash at least five years ahead of the day you'll be cashing out.

For retirees planning to live off their savings, in whole or in part, this issue is more complicated.

• Each of us has to assume we'll live to be 100, otherwise we run the risk of outliving our money.

• Since this means we might be drawing on our savings for 35 years, we can't ignore inflation risk and so need to maintain substantial exposure to stocks.

• But if we plan on withdrawing a set dollar amount for living expenses, amounting to 4% or 5% of our investment portfolio, we also can't afford to ignore market volatility.

• To solve this dilemma, I recommend that retirees in their 60s keep about 60% or so in stocks, with the rest split 50/50 between high-quality municipal bonds and short- to intermediate-term (i.e., two- to five-year) Treasuries.

• If bond yields rise in future years, I would shift this balance more to intermediate Treasuries and add some TIPS.

• When stock markets decline significantly, withdraw spending money from the Treasury and muni-bond accounts rather than sell stocks at depressed prices.

• When the stock market recovers, replenish the Treasury account and go back to taking money from stock dividends, capital appreciation, and muni-bond interest. Keep the Treasury account as your rainy-day fund.

As more and more baby boomers reach retirement age the issue of how much one can safely withdraw from savings, and what's the best way to do so, is attracting lots of attention. So I would encourage anyone wrestling with this problem to search online, where you'll be able to find numerous sensible articles on the topic.

CHAPTER 14

How to Keep Score Properly

If you don't keep score properly, you're very likely to incur significant opportunity costs, without even realizing you're doing so, and end up accumulating much less money than you could have had. For example, John (in chapter 12), would never have known how much more money he could have earned in his retirement fund if he hadn't been able to compare his results with Jane's.

If you're like most investors, your guesstimates of how well you've done are probably way off the mark. In *The Quest for Alpha*, Larry Swedroe summarizes the conclusions of a fascinating paper by two German finance professors who studied the performance of individuals with online brokerage accounts. Not only did 75% of these investors underperform relevant market indexes by wide margins, they "overestimated their own performance by an astounding 11.6 percent a year." And the worse they were as investors, the more they overestimated their returns. "In fact, while just 5 percent believed they had experienced negative returns, the reality was that 25 percent did so."[lxxiii]

Do you know your score?

BENCHMARKING

A crucial difference between institutional and individual investing is that most institutions keep score rigorously and most individuals don't. In fact, institutions spend lots of time and money developing reliable scorecards. It's called "benchmarking" and its purpose is to answer the question, "How are we doing?"

That's not as easy as it sounds. Absent any context, the obvious response to "How are we doing?" should be, "compared to what?" So well-managed institutions keep several scores, each designed to show how they are doing relative to a specific investment objective.

By comparison, the only scorecard most individuals see is one that shows them how much money they have in their account compared to last month, or last quarter, and year-to-date. Beyond this, most mutual funds and brokerage firms assiduously avoid providing you with the kind of scorecard their institutional clients demand.

For individual investors saving for some long-term goal like retirement, or a college fund for their two-year old, "How are we doing?" first means "How far along are we in accumulating the money we need?" Your mutual fund and/or brokerage statements will enable you to keep track of the growth of your savings in nominal dollar terms, but it's also instructive to see how you're doing after accounting for inflation, which you can easily compute by simply reducing the nominal dollar value each year by the trailing 12-month's CPI (Consumer Price Index), found at www.inflationdata.com. Then just keep a running tally of the inflation-adjusted value of your savings.

The next question to answer should be "How are we doing compared to our policy (or target) portfolio?" This is the portfolio you've mapped out in your investment plan as the best route to realizing your objectives. You should keep track of how it performs by recording the returns of each asset class you invest in, weighted by the percentage you have in each.

For example, if the target asset allocation for your retirement savings account is 40% in US stocks, 30% in Non-US stocks, 15% in Treasury bonds, and 15% in long-term municipal bonds, you should track the returns of a portfolio invested 40% in the S&P 500 index, 30% in the MSCI EAFE index, 15% in Barclay's Treasury Bond Index, and 15% in Barclay's municipal bond index. In this way you can measure whether your actual returns are better or worse than those of your target portfolio.

Why bother? Two reasons.

• First, this will tell you whether any deviations you make from your target asset allocation have added or detracted value.

• Secondly, if you have any active managers this will show whether they're doing any better than the benchmark indexes they're trying to beat.

Of course, sticking with your investment plan means that whenever the actual allocations of your investment portfolio deviate materially from those of the roadmap, you should rebalance back to those target allocations to get back on track.

Because active managers generally don't outperform passive index funds over time, net of fees and taxes, you generally shouldn't invest with them at all.

MUTUAL FUNDS
PERFORMANCE REPORTING

Unfortunately, mutual fund companies often don't provide you with appropriate market index benchmarks. As far as I know, none do so on clients' statements.

For example, I randomly selected two funds managed by the American Funds Group: The New Economy Fund and The Bond Fund of America. If you go to the firm's website, select one of these funds, navigate the bewildering array of different share classes, and click on "detailed fund information" you do indeed get a wealth of detail, including investment returns, but no data on these funds' performance relative to an appropriate benchmark index. For that you have to dig into the annual reports, but the benchmark comparisons there are of dubious value since the New Economy

Fund is compared to the S&P 500, although it is a global fund with extensive holdings of non-US securities, and the Bond Fund of America is compared to Barclays Capital Aggregate Bond Index, although it may invest up to 25% in non-US bonds.

Where is the SEC? Why isn't the regulatory body that is supposed to protect investors' interests requiring all mutual funds to include an appropriate benchmark index in their funds' performance reporting? As it is, some do, some don't. For example, check out the websites of TIAA-CREF, Vanguard, and Fidelity. If you select a specific fund and then click on the performance tab, you get multi-period performance, up to 10 years, shown side by side with the results of an appropriate benchmark index. That should be the industry standard and it should be enforced by the industry's regulator.

Even better would be if all funds were also required to provide after-tax performance data, which, again, some already do (e.g., Fidelity). After all, almost half of individual investors' assets are invested in taxable accounts, which means that every time a mutual fund makes a distribution, taxes take a bite out of the returns. For the most part, the mutual fund industry ignores this consideration, rarely reporting performance net of taxes and rarely managing portfolios in tax-efficient ways.

After tax-return data can be found on the website of Morningstar, one of the two major services providing data, information, analysis, and commentary on mutual funds and exchange-traded funds (ETFs).[lxxiv]

HOW TO KEEP SCORE

A proper scorecard enables you to keep track of how you are doing in multiple ways. Twenty years ago, it would have been quite difficult for individuals to construct and maintain such a scorecard. Today, however, there are software programs designed specifically for this purpose.[lxxv] Similarly, some brokerage firms have online tools that enable clients to track the performance of their holdings asset class by asset class and measure the results against those of relevant benchmark indexes (e.g., Schwab)—but all the assets have to be in accounts at that firm.

So what should your scorecard show?

1. The dollar value of your total investment portfolio. If your assets are invested in different accounts, with various firms, you obviously need to aggregate them.

2. As noted above, you should also look at the inflation-adjusted value of your portfolio each year.

3. The performance of your actual portfolio beside that of your target portfolio (using index fund data for each asset class to measure the latter).

4. The performance of each asset class beside the appropriate benchmark index. If your portfolio is invested entirely in index funds, the results will be

almost identical—minus the small fee your index fund manager charges—and this will not be necessary. Where you have active managers, the results will differ more dramatically.

The performance of each manager beside the appropriate benchmark index. For example, if your US equity portfolio consists of three different funds—perhaps a large-cap value manager, a large-cap growth manager and a small-cap manager, then their returns should be shown beside those of a US large-cap value index (e.g., the Russell 1000 Value Index), a US large-cap growth index (e.g., the Russell 1000 Growth Index), and a US small-cap index (e.g., the Russell 2000 Index).

If this sounds like a lot, actually it's not. Any well-designed performance reporting system will include all of these scores in one easily reviewable format and if you're adept at spreadsheets, you can easily create your own.

If you're not familiar with the many benchmark indexes available, you can research them easily on the web. But when selecting indexes for your performance report, keep it simple. Here are the most commonly used:

• Global Equities: If including emerging markets, the Morgan Stanley Capital International All Country World Equity Index (MSCI ACWI).

• If developed markets only, the MSCI World Equity Index (MSCI World).

- For the total US stock market, the Russell 3000 Index.

- For US large-cap, the Russell 1000 Index or the S&P 500 Index.

- For US small-cap, the Russell 2000 Index.

- For US large-cap growth, small-cap growth, large-cap value and small-cap value, the Russell 1000 Growth Index, the Russell 2000 Growth Index, the Russell 1000 Value Index, and the Russell 2000 Value Index, respectively.

- For developed equity markets outside the US, the MSCI Europe, Australia, Far East Index (MSCI EAFE).

- For emerging equity markets, the MCSI Emerging Markets Index.

- For bonds, Barclays has several US Treasury indexes and a municipal bond index—all easily accessible on the web.

If you have any cash in the actual portfolio, those returns should be included in the actual returns of the bond portfolio if the allocation to cash in your target portfolio is zero.

Of course, you can't actually invest cost-free in the MSCI ACWI or any of the other indexes cited above. So the costless indexes you track always have a small edge on your actual portfolio, even if invested entirely in index tracking funds. What are the minimum fees you would have to incur?

• For an S&P 500 or other Large-Cap US Equity index ETF or fund, 4-15 basis points.

• For a global or non-US equity index ETF or fund, 10-25 basis points.

• For an emerging markets equity index ETF or fund, 15-30 basis points.

• For bond and money market funds, 5-15 basis points.

CONCLUSION

Investment managers often pooh-pooh benchmarking as accounting mumbo-jumbo or consultant-speak that serves no useful purpose. "Our focus is on making money for our clients," they like to say. Fine, but surely we should calculate whether you're making more or less money for your clients, net of fees (and taxes) than they could be earning in some comparable investment product with the same risk and return objectives?

Anyone invested in actively managed funds (or in a managed stock or bond account) should be familiar with the terms "beta" and "alpha."

The return of a benchmark index, like the S&P 500 index of large-cap US stocks, is beta. The amount added or detracted by an active manager is alpha.

For example:

• ABC Mutual Fund invests in Large-Cap US Growth Stocks and has returned 24.5%, 2.4% and 2.9% over the past one-, three-, and five-year periods.

• Is this performance good or bad?

• Since this fund invests in Large-Cap US Growth, the appropriate benchmark is the Russell 1000 Growth Index. The companies in that index constitute the opportunity set from which the manager of the ABC fund selects stocks for his portfolio.

• So the obvious question is: did his selections add value or not? That's alpha. The index return is beta.

• Since the index returned 23.7%, 3.1%, and 3.8% over these same periods, we see that although the manager beat his benchmark last year, over the past three and five years he failed to add value, net of fees. In other words, alpha was negative.

This distinction used to be academic, because investors had no way to invest in such indexes as the Russell 1000 Growth Index. But that's no longer true. Most stock and bond indexes, both domestic and international, are now investable via low-cost index mutual funds or exchange-traded funds (ETFs).

In other words, you can buy beta cheaply, because it doesn't cost much to create and run a fund that passively buys and holds all the stocks or bonds in a given index. You don't have to pay analysts and portfolio managers, you just program a computer.

Indeed, any investment strategy that can be replicated by programming a computer should be regarded as earning beta rather than alpha returns. Let's say your strategy is to invest in US companies paying a current dividend yield of at least 3.0% that have increased the dividend every year for the past 10 years. Fine, we can easily program a computer to identify those, then buy them all and sit tight. The return from this process would be a beta return.

Or you could find an active manager who pursues a similar, dividend-oriented strategy and invest with her in hopes that she can add value, net of the higher fees, from judicious stock selection. The difference between her fund's return and the computer's passive selection is alpha.

Bottom line? If you're invested in actively managed funds, or actively managed stock or bond accounts, you should know whether your managers are generating any value-added (alpha) or not—because that's what you're paying them for.

As detailed in the chapter on active management, all managers promise positive alpha, but pitifully few consistently deliver—not because they're stupid or incompetent, but because all these very smart people are competing against each other in a brutally efficient market, and their efforts to outperform the relevant market indexes are hobbled by the fees they charge.

So don't simply look at your account statement to see if you have more or less money in your portfolio than you did last quarter or last year. Take the time to set up a proper performance measurement report so that you are getting the feedback you need about your investment choices to determine whether these are adding value or not. Otherwise you'll probably end up incurring significant opportunity costs that will leave you considerably poorer than you would have been if you'd kept score properly.

Conclusion

The superior man understands what is right; the inferior man understands what will sell.

Confucius

In the financial markets, what you don't know can hurt you badly. So you should either learn what you need to know to invest successfully or hire someone else to do the job for you.

And even if your investable assets amount to as little as $25,000 today, you can now get some good advice, at low cost, from online firms like Wealthfront.com and Betterment.com.

If you want a local advisor, with whom you can meet face-to-face, and who'll provide you with integrated financial and investment planning services, you'll probably have to wait until you've accumulated more money in your accounts, since such firms generally have much higher minimums.

DOING IT YOURSELF

If you're just starting out on an investment program or have decided to go it alone, you need to understand the following:

Behavioral Risk

• As investors we are frequently our own worst enemy, because we're programmed to respond to bull and bear markets in exactly the wrong way.

• If the stock market has been rising strongly in recent years, we feel safe and comfortable when we should realize that the risk of a serious decline increases with every uptick in the Dow Jones.

• And when markets tank, every instinct we have tells us to flee, although this is in fact the best time for long-term investors to commit more to the market.

• So you need some *objective* metrics and mechanisms to stop yourself from following your instincts. The best defense is knowledge of capital markets history and some understanding of stock market valuations.

Financial Services Industry

• Most investors don't buy investment products like mutual funds by themselves; they are *sold* such products by the financial services industry.

• Most individuals and companies in the financial services industry work within incentives to make money from you, not for you.

• Indeed, research has shown that hundreds of billions of dollars flow each year from investors to the financial services industry with no commensurate value added. In fact, value added isn't zero; it's negative.

• This is because investors have been sold three propositions that have long since been proved false by a mountain of independent research:

> ➤ The first is that active managers outperform the market. They don't. In any given period, 2/3 of actively managed stock mutual funds underperform the market—and they do so, on average, by a larger margin than that of those who outperform.

> ➤ The second proposition is that you, we, someone, can identify in advance which managers will outperform. You, we, someone can't. Above all,

past performance is not predictive of future performance.

> The third false proposition is that financial gurus can forecast the stock market's performance, the direction of interest rates, the rate of inflation, GDP growth, and so on. They can't. There is no evidence whatsoever that any of those high-priced experts can do better than you could do flipping a coin. This means that you should not move your investments around in response to such predictions—you'll just waste money.

• What is predictive of future performance in stock and bond funds is cost: on average, low-cost funds perform better than high-cost funds. Investors typically underestimate the impact of costs on their cumulative wealth. One of the best investment decisions you can make is to avoid relatively costly options.

• For both these reasons, you should invest in low-cost, passive index funds and ETFs, not higher-cost actively managed funds promoted by the financial services industry. In the long run, you will earn more, at less risk and much less expense.

• You should never invest in hedge funds or private equity offerings, whether directly or through funds-of-funds.

These are very high cost and net of those costs it's extremely unlikely any such funds available to individual investors will actually outperform a plain vanilla stock-bond portfolio invested in index funds.

GETTING PROFESSIONAL HELP

• The right kind of investment advisory firm will charge you a fee calculated as a percentage of the assets you entrust to them.

• This should not exceed 1.25%, should be less than that for amounts more than, say, $500,000, and should decline as the value of your assets increases. Yes, this fee is too high for the relatively little work required each year once all the initial spade-work has been completed. But it's the going rate, and for most people still a better alternative than going it alone. If you don't feel you need personal face-time with your advisor, lower-cost alternatives (for assets over $500,000) are Vanguard and Rick Ferri's firm, Portfolio Solutions.

• You can also get competent, low-cost investment advice from online firms.

• Many capable investment advisors are also financial planners, but not all financial planners are capable investment advisors.

• Many brokerage firms, wealth management firms, banks, insurance companies, and mutual funds characterize their sales reps as "financial advisors," but you should not invest with any such companies.

• The criteria for selecting a financial advisor are these:

➤ They charge fees based on assets under management. No commissions on product sales and no wrap accounts.

➤ A clean sheet on their ADV item 11, where they have to declare any misdeeds on their record. ADV information is readily available at www.adviserinfo.sec.gov.

➤ Also on the ADV, items 5F (1) should be checked "Yes", and assets under management shown in 5F (2) should substantially exceed $25 million. 5G (2) should also be checked. If these are not checked as indicated, this firm does not really have investment advisory credentials, as opposed to financial planning expertise.

➤ A coherent investment philosophy implemented entirely or at least predominantly through investments in low-cost index funds and ETFs.

➤ As a first step, they will review your financial circumstances and develop with you a written statement of investment policies and objectives.

➤ Generally, they do not have custody of your assets, which should be held at a third party custodian like Schwab, Pershing, Fidelity.

INVESTMENT PLANNING AND ASSET ALLOCATION

Whether you go it alone or hire an investment advisor, you need a *written* investment plan that charts your course towards your objectives. If you don't write this down, you will almost certainly fail to stick to your investment program when hard times hit and bear market losses have your stomach churning. So map your course, and stay with it.

How your savings are allocated across different asset classes should be determined primary by two factors:

1. Your time horizon:

➤ When will you need the money?

➤ The longer your time horizon, the more you should allocate to stocks.

➤ The shorter your time horizon, the more you should allocate to cash and bonds.

2. Your risk tolerance.

➤ If your employment and income are highly dependent on the state of the economy in general, and the financial sector in particular, then you should allocate less to stocks.

➤ If, on the other hand, you are a tenured professor of, say, biology, whose income is reasonably insulated from economic turmoil, you should have a greater tolerance for stock market risk.

➤ In other words, the stability and security of your own earning power should be incorporated into your financial plan.

➤ And you should *not* double your bets by investing heavily in your own employer's stock, or even in companies in your same industry. Otherwise you're imprudently increasing your exposure to just one sector of the economy.

➤ And if you are temperamentally incapable of weathering periodic storms of stock market volatility, you should allocate less to stocks than you otherwise might.

KEEPING SCORE

You should also keep score properly. It's not enough to know just how much money you've accumulated compared to last month or last year. You also need to know if you're ahead or behind schedule in making progress towards your goals.

In addition, you should measure your results against those of appropriate benchmark indexes. However, if you are invested in index funds, as you should be, this is less necessary.

SUMMARY

Investing need not be complicated, but it's never easy. So my concluding advice is:

- Think hard about whether you should really go it alone, or get professional help.

- Either way, with help or without, you must map your course so you know where you are going and when you plan to get there.

- Stick to your plan by rebalancing back to your target asset allocations.

- Ignore the constant noise about financial markets blaring at you 24/7.

- Keep it simple.

- Stay well away from the many predators that populate the financial services industry.

- Minimize costs.

- Invest mostly in low-cost index funds and ETFs.

Appendix

Letter to HR about your 401(k)

Dear _____,

I'm writing to request that our company review its 401(k) plan options. Our current 401(k) plan is with ABC, which offers us x investment choices. Unfortunately, all of these are high-cost, actively managed funds that generally haven't, and are never likely to, match the returns of the market indexes against which their performance should be measured. This means that our employees are paying ABC substantial fees every year for poor investment results. As you are probably already aware, new rules from the Department of Labor require plan sponsors to disclose to plan participants the amount they pay in fees and other charges per $1,000 invested. This is likely to show that our costs are relatively high, perhaps above the median 401(k) expense ratio of 0.78%, and certainly well above the 0.30% or so of lower-cost providers.

Investment experts stress that two keys to long-term investment success are controlling costs and avoiding unnecessary risk. With ABC we are incurring both high costs and the risk that their mutual funds will continue to underperform. There is no good reason to think this will change: ABC is in the business of earning as much as it can from its clients and for its shareholders. I just don't see why we should continue to contribute to their earnings.

Instead, I'd like to suggest that we consider transferring our 401(k) plan to Schwab, Fidelity Investments, or the Vanguard Group, all of which offer retirement plan participants low-cost index funds as well as actively managed options. Over time, we would all save a bundle and have a much higher probability of earning good returns on our 401(k) investments.

Yours sincerely,

Glossary

Active management Active managers attempt to outperform their benchmark through active stock selection, sector rotation, market timing, and so on. In contrast, passive managers make no such "active" decisions by investing in index funds (e.g., S&P 500 index).

Alpha The difference (positive or negative) between the return generated by an active manager and that of the benchmark index the manager is attempting to outperform.

Annualize To convert a return of any period length to an estimated annual return.

Back-end load A commission paid when an individual sells shares in a mutual fund within a certain number of years. The back-end load is intended to discourage withdrawals.

Benchmark index A standard against which an investor can evaluate a fund or portfolio's performance. For example, a suitable benchmark index against which to evaluate a large-cap US equity fund is the S&P 500 index.

Beta The return available to investors from passive index funds or ETFs.

Bid-Ask spread The difference between the lowest price a seller is willing to accept for a security (ask price) and the highest price a buyer is willing to pay for the security (bid price).

Book Value The value of a company's assets minus its liabilities.

Broker dealer/Broker A broker dealer is a firm authorized to buy, sell, and trade securities (e.g., stocks and bonds) and to sell investment products to investors. A broker is a representative of a broker dealer.

Capital gain/loss A capital gain results when the price of a security exceeds the original purchase price. A capital loss is the opposite. Note: the gain/loss remains "unrealized" until the asset is actually sold.

Capital gains distributions Payments made to mutual fund shareholders from the profits realized on the sale of securities. Distributions are typically made at the end of the calendar year and are taxable at differing rates depending on how long the fund owned the sold security. Investors in the fund at the time the distribution is made are liable for the taxes on the distribution regardless of how long they have owned the fund. Some funds permit automatic reinvestment of capital gains, but investors reinvesting their capital gains must still pay tax on them.

Cash investments Highly liquid, low-risk investments that preserve capital but offer very low returns. Examples include Treasury bills, money-market funds and short-term certificates of deposit.

Closed-end fund A fund that raises a fixed amount of money from investors to invest in a given asset class (e.g., US equities, international bonds) and subsequently trades its shares on a stock exchange. This contrasts with an open-ended fund, which typically continues to sell shares to investors after the initial offering and does not list on a stock exchange. Whereas an open-ended fund must compute its net asset value at the end of every day by simply adding up the value of its holdings, a closed-end fund may trade on the exchange for more or less than the net asset value of its holdings, since its price is determined by investor demand.

Commodities Physical substances; e.g., precious metals, grains, coal, iron ore.

Consumer Price Index (CPI) The Consumer Price Index (CPI) is a measure of the average change over time in the prices paid by urban consumers for a market basket of consumer goods and services. The CPI is the most widely used measure of inflation.

Coupon/coupon rate Bond trading is now entirely electronic, but in the past bond investors received a book of coupons, each of which stated the amount of interest the bond paid. Investors clipped these coupons every six months and sent them to the bond issuer's custodial bank or broker, which then sent payment in return. For this reason, the initial rate of interest of a bond issue is still referred to as the coupon or coupon rate.

Credit rating A rating assigned to a company, and especially to its bonds, by a rating agency like Standard and Poor's or Moody's.

Credit risk The possibility that a borrower may fail to repay.

Currency risk The possibility that a change in currency exchange rates might diminish the value of an investment denominated in a foreign currency.

Custodian A bank or brokerage firm that holds securities and implements buy and sell orders for investors.

Derivative A security whose value is derived from the price of another, underlying asset.

Dividend yield A security's dividend per share divided by its price per share.

Earnings per share A company's total earnings divided by its number of outstanding shares.

Efficient Market A market is characterized as "efficient" if all investors have equal access to all material information affecting the value of the securities traded on that market. The more efficient a market, the greater difficulty active managers have outperforming market indexes, since they have no informational advantage over other investors.

Enhanced index fund A fund that attempts to add some value to an index fund investment through a trading strategy (e.g., instead of buying all the shares in the S&P 500 index itself, buy the S&P 500 futures and invest the requisite collateral in 2-year Treasury bonds rather than in 30-day Treasury bills).

Exchange-Traded Fund (ETF) An investment fund traded on stock exchanges. Originally designed as closed-end funds invested in simple index products (e.g., the Barclay's Aggregate Bond Index, the S&P 500 Index), ETFs are now invested in many different ways.

Expense ratio The percentage of a fund's assets that go toward the costs of operating the fund, including the management fee. These expenses lower the returns to the fund's investors.

Fee-only advisor An investment advisor or financial planner that does not earn commissions on investment or financial (e.g., insurance company) products sold to clients, but is compensated solely by the fees he or she charges. Investors (and those seeking financial planning advice) should generally deal only with fee-only advisors.

Front-end load A commission or sales fee paid by an investor to a third-party (an investment advisor or broker) at the time shares are purchased.

Fund family A group of mutual funds offered by one company. Typically, the fund offerings cover a range of investment objectives; e.g., large- and small-cap US stocks, international stocks and bonds, money-market funds.

Global fund A mutual fund that invests in companies throughout the world.

Gross Domestic Product (GDP) The market value of all officially recognized final goods and services produced within a country in a given period.

Hedge fund The only common denominator among hedge funds is high fees (typically 2% of assets and 20% of profits) and a legal structure defining the relationship between the manager of the fund (the general partner) and the fund's investors (the limited partners). Other than these common factors, hedge funds have widely varied investment mandates and objectives, from relatively conservative to highly aggressive.

High-yield fund A fund investing in bonds rated below "investment grade"; i.e., rated "B" or lower.

Index provider An investment firm that offers investors passive index funds.

Indexing The (highly recommended) practice of investing in low-cost passive index funds rather than in higher-cost actively managed funds.

Inflation risk The possibility that the value of an investment will be eroded by inflation.

Interest-rate risk The possibility that the value of an interest-bearing asset (bond) will decline as interest rates rise.

International fund A fund investing in stocks or bonds of countries other than the US

Investment advisor An individual, firm, or committee responsible for making investment decisions on behalf of clients.

Investment-grade bond A medium- to high-rated bond that indicates that the issuer is deemed by credit rating agencies to have a low risk of default.

Junk bond The lowest grade of high-yield bonds.

Large-cap stocks are stocks of companies with a market capitalization greater than $10 billion.

Load fund A mutual fund that charges commission fees to investors when they buy or sell fund shares. Since there is no evidence that such funds perform better than no-load funds, investors should never buy load funds.

Long-term capital gain The profit from the sale of a qualifying investment held for more than 12 months and then sold. Long-term capital gains are typically subject to a lower federal tax rate than are short-term capital gains.

Management fee The fee charged by an investment fund or investment advisor to manage an investor's assets.

Market capitalization The capitalization of a company is equal to the total number of shares outstanding times the current share price.

Maturity/Maturity date The date a bond issuer must repay investors their principal.

Mid-cap Mid-cap companies are those with a capitalization of approximately $2 billion to $10 billion.

Momentum investing An investment strategy based on the theory that security (or sector or market) that has gone up in price will keep appreciating while one that has dropped in price will continue to decline. Although research has shown some evidence of short-term momentum in individual stocks and markets, investors who attempt to invest on the basis of momentum typically come to grief.

Municipal bond A bond issued by a government entity below the federal level; e.g., a state, city, county, school district, public utility, to raise funds for infrastructure projects like road improvements and school construction. Municipal bonds are exempt from federal taxes and if the investor resides in the state in which the bonds have been issued they will also be exempt from most state and local taxes.

No-load fund A mutual fund that does not charge investors when they buy or sell shares in the fund.

Nominal return The rate of return on an investment without adjustment for inflation.

Open-end fund See the definition of closed-end fund, above.

Operating expenses Costs incurred in the normal course of business, including employee salaries, research and development, and legal and accounting fees.

Overlap The extent to which the holdings of an actively managed fund overlap with those of a benchmark index. For example, if the manager of an actively managed US stock fund owns the same shares as are in the S&P 500 index, in the same quantities, then he has 100% overlap with the index and therefore his performance will mirror that of the index (minus the manager's fee). The more a manager's holdings overlap with those of a benchmark index, the more those holdings that are different from those in the index must outperform the index for the total fund to post a better return than that of the index. For example, if a US stock fund manager's holdings overlap with those of the S&P 500 by 85%, then 85% of the fund will post the same return as that of the index, while the 15% that is different will post a better or worse return. The question is: how much better must the return of that 15% be to make up for the manager's fee? (which is, of course, levied on 100% of the assets in the fund.)

Passive management The only completely passive portfolio is the global portfolio of all assets, public and private. In practice, therefore, all investors must make some active decisions, even if those are decisions not to hold certain asset classes. In common usage, however, passive investing is often equated with indexing and in this context, it means investing with a manager whose sole objective is to match the performance of a given benchmark index at very low cost.

Portfolio transaction costs The costs of buying and selling securities in a portfolio or fund.

Price-to-Earnings ratio A ratio of a stock's price per share divided by its earnings per share. There are several versions of the P/E ratio, depending on what kinds of earnings are used as the denominator. For example, reported or operating earnings, trailing 12-month or 10-year average earnings (aka "normalized" earnings).

Real Estate Investment Trust (REIT) A company that owns and usually operates income-producing real estate like hotels, apartment buildings, shopping malls, hospitals, offices, etc. The difference between a REIT and a company whose business is building, buying, and managing property is that a REIT is not taxed at the corporate level, but must distribute at least 90% of its income to shareholders, who are then liable for income tax on these distributions. Shares of many REITs are traded on major exchanges and individual investors may invest in individual REITS or in REIT mutual funds.

Real return A real return is the nominal or actual return adjusted for inflation. It is calculated using the following formula: $(1 + \text{nominal return}) / (1 + \text{inflation rate}) = (1 + \text{real return})$. For example, if the nominal return were 10% and the inflation rate 4%, then the real return would be 5.8%.

Registered investment advisor Anyone earning fees or commissions from investment advice offered to clients must register with the SEC or state authorities as a registered investment advisor and provide information about their business on form ADV. Representatives of brokerage firms (who are often labeled "financial advisors" or "investment consultants") are not required to register since they are—notwithstanding their titles—sales representatives masquerading as investment advisors.

Risk premium The excess return investors expect to earn from a higher-risk investment (e.g., stocks versus bonds) to compensate for the greater risk of loss.

Risk tolerance The extent to which an investor will accept declines in the value of his/her portfolio.

Sector fund A mutual fund that invests exclusively in companies from a particular industry or sector of the economy; e.g., technology or financials.

Securities and Exchange Commission (SEC) The federal agency charged with regulating the securities industry and enforcing federal securities law. The SEC requires public companies to submit a range of reports on their financial performance and the online EDGAR database makes this information available to investors. Similarly, the SEC (and state regulators) require any firm offering investment advice to file form ADV, which is accessible to investors online.

Short-term capital gain The profit from the sale of a qualifying investment held for less than 12 months and then sold. Short-term capital gains are taxed as ordinary income.

Small cap The capitalization of a company is equal to the total number of shares outstanding times the current share price. The terms "small cap", "mid cap" and "large cap" are very flexible, but as a rough guide, small cap would be up to $2 billion, mid-cap $2 billion to $10 billion, and large-cap in excess of $10 billion.

Standard deviation A statistical measure of the volatility of returns for an investment

Tax-exempt bond See Municipal Bond, above.

Total return The change in the market value of an investment, plus income, divided by the starting market value.

Treasury Inflation-Protected Securities (TIPS) Treasury bonds indexed to the Consumer Price Index to protect the bondholder from inflation risk.

Treasury securities Government debt issued by the US Dept. of Treasury, including Treasury bills, Treasury notes, Treasury bonds, and Treasury Inflation-Protected Securities.

12b-1 fee A fee charged by some mutual funds to pay for marketing and advertising expenses, including payments to brokers who sell the fund shares. The fee is named for a section in the Investment Company Act of 1940. Investors should not buy funds that levy 12b-1 fees.

Unrealized capital gain/loss Change in the value of a security that has not yet been sold. The gain is "realized" when the security is sold.

Volatility A statistical measure of the dispersion of returns for a security.

Wrap fee A wrap fee is an annual fee calculated as a percentage of assets in an account at a brokerage firm (e.g., Morgan Stanley, Merrill Lynch, J.P. Morgan, Raymond James). Investors should never hold assets in any account that charges such a fee.

Yield-to-Maturity A calculation of the rate of return on a bond if it is held until maturity.

Recommended Readings

A quick search on Amazon.com brings up hundreds of books on investing. You could spend years reading them all and end up thoroughly confused by their conflicting advice. So this list covers a tiny sliver of that total universe, consisting only of a few books I have both read and consider well worth recommending. Unlike conventional bibliographies it isn't organized alphabetically, but in order of priority; that is, the books I consider *most* valuable to individual investors are listed first.

Daniel C. Goldie & Gordon S. Murray, *The Investment Answer*. Business Plus, The Hachette Book Group, 2011.

Listed first for one major reason: brevity. In about 70 generously spaced pages, this primer provides novice investors with a clear, cogent, reliable guide to everything they need to know to invest successfully. Goldie and Murray boil everything down to five key decisions:

1. Invest on your own or hire an advisor? If hiring an advisor, how to choose the right one.

2. How to allocate your investments among different asset classes.

3. How to diversify your portfolio.

4. Should your investments be allocated to actively managed or to passive strategies?

5. When and how should you rebalance back to your target allocation by selling some investments and buying others?

These are indeed key questions and the authors answer them clearly, succinctly and wisely.

In short, this is an ideal guide for busy people not much interested in devoting time to more detailed (and sometimes ponderous) investment tomes.

**Jason Zweig, *The Little Book of Safe Money.*
John Wiley & Sons, 2010.**

As William Bernstein writes in his foreword to this excellent guide, Jason Zweig's expertise extends from investment theory to capital markets history to "the cognitive neuropsychological aspects of finance." In just over 220 pages of sparkling prose, *The Little Book of Safe Money* gives readers a wealth of sound financial planning and investment advice, with many useful references to websites where readers can find additional material, financial planning tools, and so on. I list Goldie & Murray's book first, only because it's so admirably brief, but I would recommend Zweig's book to everyone trying to save and invest for the future.

Charles D. Ellis, *Winning the Loser's Game*, fifth edition. McGraw Hill, 2010.

At 200 breezy pages, this timeless classic is now in its fifth edition and remains one of the best books ever written about investing. It should be read by anyone interested in the subject and/or going it alone. At the heart of Ellis' advice is his insight that individual investors can succeed only if they refuse to play a game rigged against them. "Winning the loser's game of beating the market is easy: *Don't play it.*" Instead, Ellis shows how you can win by developing and implementing a sound investment plan designed to realize your objectives.

Larry E. Swedroe, *The Only Guide You'll Ever Need for the Right Financial Plan*. Bloomberg Press, 2010.

This is an excellent primer on the integration of financial planning and investing. Swedroe explains financial and investment products with admirable clarity, giving sound advice on which products to include in your investment plan and which to avoid. Unlike most books on investing, *The Only Guide* also gives advice on College Savings Plans, Annuities, Long-Term Care Insurance, Life Settlements, traditional and Roth IRAs, Social Security, and reverse mortgages.

In short, readers looking for financial planning advice as much as for investment advice might do well to start here.

William J. Bernstein, *The Investor's Manifesto.* John Wiley & Sons, 2010.

In contrast, this is very much a book for those specifically interested in investing. William Bernstein is one of the best thinkers in the investment business, and although he makes more demands on his readers than do any of the authors already listed, his writing is admirably witty and clear. He notes that successful investors must be interested in the process of investing, must have some mathematical ability allied with a knowledge of financial history, and must be highly disciplined. He believes few people possess these necessary qualities in sufficient measure and that they would therefore be better off having someone else manage their money. Like all the authors in this list, however, he warns readers against the "muggers and worse" of the financial services industry: "The prudent investor treats almost the entirety of the financial industrial landscape as an urban combat zone."

Full of intelligent advice and valuable information, this book also combines the virtues of brevity and clarity.

Richard A. Ferri, *The Power of Passive Investing.*
John Wiley & Sons, 2011.

Larry E. Swedroe, *The Quest for Alpha.*
John Wiley & Sons, 2011.

Both these books detail the reams of research puncturing the myth perpetuated by the financial services industry that you, or your broker, or the mutual funds they want to sell you can "beat the market." Ferri's is more comprehensive and serves as an excellent resource for anyone wanting to dig into this subject and understand the rationale for index fund investing in detail. Swedroe's book is considerably shorter and includes more detail on the failures of hedge funds and private equity managers (both venture capital and buyout) to deliver value added to their investors.

Either or both should be required reading for anyone whose money is managed by a "wealth management" firm or invested in actively managed mutual funds.

David F. Swensen, *Unconventional Success.*
Free Press, 2005.

Swensen, who is Yale University's chief investment officer, set out to instruct individual investors how they could copy the investment blueprint for endowment funds laid out in his earlier book, *Pioneering Portfolio Management.* However, when he examined the resources available to individuals, and the research on retail investing, he came to realize this was completely unrealistic. Consequently, *Unconventional Success* actually provides the same advice as all the books listed above: steer clear of brokers, commission-driven "financial advisors," wrap-fee accounts and actively-managed mutual funds.

Like Ellis and Swedroe, he warns individual investors to steer clear of private equity investments (e.g., venture capital and buyout funds) and hedge funds, showing just how poorly retail investors in such asset classes have fared.

What distinguishes Swensen's book is not therefore the advice he offers, but the venom he directs at the mutual fund industry for its habitual fleecing of unsuspecting investors. More than any of the works above, he details the mendacity and larceny of firms cited by the SEC for unscrupulous business practices and excoriates the industry for disservice to its customers. Ellis, Swedroe, and Bernstein take the same view, with Bernstein the most caustic of those three, but none launches a diatribe as bitter as Swensen's.

Unconventional Success is full of useful data and sensible advice, but at 370 pages makes considerable demands on readers' time and attention.

John C. Bogle, *Common Sense on Mutual Funds*, 10th Anniversary Edition. John Wiley & Sons, 2010.

No recommended reading list of investment books for individual investors would be complete without at least one work by Jack Bogle, founder of Vanguard, scourge of the financial services industry, and tireless advocate for index fund investing. *Common Sense on Mutual Funds* is classic Bogle, packed full of excellent research, analysis and advice, but weighing in at over 600 pages, it's definitely for readers prepared to invest a good deal of time and energy deepening their knowledge of investing. More succinct and accessible is Bogle's *The Little Book of Common Sense Investing*, published by Wiley in 2007.

Notes

Introduction

[i] Cambridge Associates is a privately held independent consulting firm providing consulting and investment oversight to more than 900 clients worldwide from eight offices across three continents. It provides clients with unbiased advice based on intensive and independent research on capital markets and investment managers.

[ii] See the glossary for definition of "asset class." Briefly, however, an asset class is simply a type of investment, like stocks or bonds or cash. These are all "asset classes."

[iii] A company's market capitalization is computed by multiplying the number of its shares by the price per share. For example, the US industrial company DuPont has 937,039,000 shares outstanding, and so if its price per share is $47.60, its market capitalization is (in round numbers) $44,603,000,000.

[iv] A mutual fund and an ETF both consist of a basket of stocks (or bonds), selected according to some criteria. But whereas you can buy and sell an ETF on a stock exchange at any time, at whatever price it is then trading, mutual fund shares do not trade on any stock exchange, and their prices are computed once a day at the end of the day. So if you place an order to buy ABC mutual fund at 10:00 a.m., you don't know what price you will pay, since that won't be computed until the end of the day (i.e., 4:00 p.m.).

[v] For example, in November 2012, Hewlett Packard was in deep trouble, with the stock selling at $11.64, having declined 56% since the beginning of the year. In contrast, Apple had become the most valuable company in the world, widely admired,

with a stock selling at $571.91, having appreciated 40% since the start of 2012 (but down from its peak of $702.41 on September 21st). Fast forward to May 31, 2013: Hewlett Packard seems to be recovering, and its stock is now selling at $25.15, up 116% from its November low. In contrast, Apple's stock has declined 21% to $452.50 from its price on that same date, and 36% in the eight months since its September 2012 peak.

Chapter 1: Do It Yourself or Hire an Advisor?

[vi] Walter Updegrave, "Should I Hire a Financial Adviser or Go It Alone?" CNNMoney.com, November 29, 2011.

[vii] AdvisEr or AdvisOr? Same, same, no different; -er is more common in American English and -or in British, but each is used on both sides of the pond.

[viii] Charles D. Ellis, *Winning the Loser's Game*, Fifth Edition. McGraw Hill, 2010.

[ix] Which can be easily checked out. See not only www.adviserinflo.sec.gov, which is discussed in detail below, but also www.finra.org/brokercheck, www.cfp.net/search (for checking on financial planners), and www.nasaa.org.

[x] Tom Stabile, "Wealth managers' big, dirty secret," *Financial Times*, June 6, 2011.

[xi] But see Jason Zweig's, "Risky Business: The Quiz That Could Steer You Wrong," in *The Wall Street Journal*, May 3, 2013 on risk-tolerance questionnaires favored by financial and investment advisors: "Many of these questionnaires are unhelpful at best and harmful at worst."

[xii] Staff turnover at large firms is also a persistent problem. For example, according to the *New York Times*, since the 2008 financial crisis the giant Swiss bank UBS has shed 1,000 of the 8,000 "advisors" it had employed in its wealth management division.

[xiii] This may change. The SEC is considering a new regulation requiring brokers and advisors to become fiduciaries.

Chapter 2: How to Go It Alone

[xiv] See the glossary for definition of "asset class." Briefly, however, an asset class is simply a type of investment, like stocks or bonds or cash.

xv Many states also offer 529 college savings plans. But not all have been wisely managed: see chapter ten, "How to Get Your Kids through College without Going Broke," in Jason Zweig's *The Little Book of Safe Money*. John Wiley & Sons, 2010.

Chapter 3: The Capital Markets

xvi Data in the table are from *Credit Suisse Global Investment Returns Sourcebook 2013*, edited by Elroy Dimson, Paul Marsh and Mike Staunton. Where no source citation is given for subsequent data, they are from Cambridge Associates.

xvii "On the Nature of Returns," in *Common Sense on Mutual Funds*, 10th Anniversary Edition. John Wiley & Sons, 2010. Bogle's formula for fundamental returns is the sum of starting dividend yield + real earnings growth, but it is more accurate to characterize this as starting dividend yield + real dividend growth. However, earnings growth data are more readily available and can serve as a reasonable proxy (as in the section below on the composition of stock market returns).

xviii Peris, *The Strategic Dividend Investor*. McGraw Hill, 2011, pp. 26-27 and 56.

xix Manufacturing now accounts for only 12% of US GDP.

xx The CAPE is easily accessible via the web at www.econ.yale.edu/~shiller/data.htm. Here you will find online valuation data and also an invaluable Excel file, which you can download, giving monthly data since January 1871 for US stock market prices, dividends, and earnings per share, plus the consumer price index (so that the nominal data can be inflation-adjusted).

xxi By mid-2007, the earnings of the financial sector comprised more than 40% of S&P500 earnings, and financial sector earnings fell deeply into negative territory in the crash of 2008-09.

xxii Quoted by Peris in *The Strategic Dividend Investor*.

xxiii According to Daniel Kahneman, a behavioral psychologist who won the Nobel prize in economics, 81% of US entrepreneurs launching a new business venture put their odds of success at 70%, despite the harsh reality that 65% of US small business start-ups fail within five years.

xxiv I'm indebted to Jason Zweig's *The Little Book of Safe Money* for this reference.

ˣˣᵛ Daniel C. Goldie & Gordon S. Murray, *The Investment Answer*. Business Plus, Hachette Book Group, 2011, p. 61.

ˣˣᵛⁱ A *New York Times* article of 12/11/2011 reports that "study after study shows that most hedge funds either lose money or make tepid returns. Many—and some argue, most—actually shut down after a few years."

ˣˣᵛⁱⁱ For a thorough dissection of this subject see Simon Lack's, *The Hedge Fund Mirage*. See also Mark Hulbert's *Wall Street Journal* column of May 31, 2013, "The Verdict Is In: Hedge Funds Aren't Worth the Money."

ˣˣᵛⁱⁱⁱ In the credit crunch of 2007-08, high-quality corporate bonds also dropped in price, despite a sharp drop in interest rates, because these were the only bonds leveraged investors could actually sell to raise cash to meet margin calls. The market in high-yield, or junk bonds simply shut down for several months as liquidity evaporated. This prolonged lack of liquidity in the bond markets was, however, unprecedented.

ˣˣⁱˣ Treasury bills have maturities of no more than 12 months and are issued at a discount to face value such that investors' return comes from the difference between the offering price (e.g., $975) and the price at maturity (e.g., $1000). Treasury notes are issues with maturities from one to ten years, and Treasury bonds are issues with maturities longer than ten years. Collectively, these are all referred to as "Treasuries."

ˣˣˣ These are Standard & Poor's ratings. Moody's system is virtually identical.

ˣˣˣⁱ Example: Your friendly local broker calls with a "special commission-free offer" of ten Arlington County, Virginia school bonds, maturing in 2020, with a 6% coupon, priced at $15,000 to yield 4.0%, free of both Virginia and Federal taxes. So you buy the bonds, but decide a week later that you have to sell them to buy your son a used car. Interest rates haven't budged, but the offer you get from the brokerage firm is $14,200, or 5.33% less than you paid. That $800 difference is the "bid-ask" spread, and is where the brokerage firm and their salesmen make their money.

Chapter 4: Forecasts Are Worthless

ˣˣˣⁱⁱ The only exception to this accurate indictment is a private New York think tank called the Economic Cycle Research Institute, which has a remarkably good record of predicting the onset of US economic recessions.

xxxiii James Montier, *The Little Book of Behavioral Investing*, John Wiley & Sons, 2010, pp. 59-60.

xxxiv See Rick Ferri, "Gurus are Still Wrong After 80 Years," posted 2/8/2011 on Rick Ferri's website: www.rickferri.com. His book is *The Power of Passive Investing*, (John Wiley & Sons, Inc.), 2011. Ferri is the founder of the investment firm, Portfolio Solutions, as well as an investment author and columnist.

xxxv Quoted in Jason Zweig, *Your Money and Your Brain*, Simon & Shuster, (2007), p. 76. Highly recommended for anyone interested in behavioral finance.

Chapter 5: Market Timing Doesn't Pay

xxxvi Bogle, *Common Sense on Mutual Funds*, p. 28.

Chapter 6: It's Not the Growth Rate, Stupid—It's the Price

xxxvii William Bernstein, *The Investor's Manifesto*, John Wiley & Sons, 2010.

xxxviii Data from William Bernstein's *The Investor's Manifesto*, p. 28.

Chapter 7: Turn Off CNBC

xxxix Ellis, *Winning the Loser's Game*, p.29.

xl Goldie & Murray, *The Investment Answer*, p. 31.

xli David Swensen, *Unconventional Success: A Fundamental Approach to Personal Investment*, Free Press, 2005, p. 169.

xlii Ron Lieber, "Resisting the Urge to Run Away from Home," *The New York Times*, August 6, 2011. Lieber's columns consistently offer sensible and useful advice, on both investing and financial planning issues.

xliii Ellis, *Winning the Loser's Game*, pp. 30-31.

xliv Bernstein, *The Investor's Manifesto*, p. 117.

Chapter 8: The Financial Services Industry Is Looking for You, Chump

xlv *The Continuing Evolution of the Mutual Fund Industry*, 1995, and updated 1998.

xlvi "The wide-ranging report, Financial Markets 2020, is based on a survey of more than 2,600 industry participants and government officials across 84 countries." Reported in the *Financial Times* on April 3, 2011.

xlvii This paper can be found at http://mba.tuck.dartmouth.edu/pages/faculty/ken.french/.

xlviii Graham Bowley and Julie Creswell, "Stock Pickers Are No Longer the Stars," *New York Times*, August 9, 2011.

xlix David Swensen's *Unconventional Success* (Free Press, 2005) documents numerous examples of unethical and/or predatory conduct by financial service firms.

l Two exceptions to this are Vanguard and TIAA-CREF, which are non-profit organizations—a major reason why they can offer lower-cost products than for-profit competitors.

li Research has shown that "we tend to discount disclosed conflicts of interest and, in general, underestimate their importance." From *The New Yorker*, 5/3/2011, p.25. The research is that of George Lowenstein of Carnegie-Mellon University.

lii This brief talk, "Putting Investors First," is recommended reading and can be found at www.jasonzweig.com, in the section on speeches.

liii Dig into the archives of Forbes magazine for classic accounts of such infamous firms as First Jersey Securities (July 16, 1984) and Blinder Robinson (April 20, 1987), which both scammed investors for years before being shut down.

liv "Market economies are always vulnerable to chancers and spivs who sell overpriced goods to ill-informed customers and seem to promise things they do not intend to deliver. If such behaviour becomes a dominant business style, you end up with the economies of

Nigeria and Haiti, where rampant opportunism makes it almost prohibitively difficult for honest people to do business." John Kay, *Financial Times*, 5/11/2011.

lv Sometimes euphemistically characterized as a "placement fee."

Chapter 9: Active Fund Management: There's No Value Added

lvi Flows of money into and out of equity mutual funds are heavily influenced by Morningstar ratings, which rank funds into quintiles on the basis of their risk-adjusted performance in recent years. As numerous commentators—and, perversely, Morningstar itself—have pointed out, this is very unfortunate since there's absolutely no evidence that five-star funds (i.e., those in the top quintile) subsequently outperform those in lower quintiles. Morningstar's own analysis shows that the main determinant of a fund's future performance is its expense ratio, not its past performance. In other words, the only prediction investors can take to the bank is that lower cost funds will outperform higher cost funds.

lvii For those interested in pursuing this topic, see http://finance.martinsewell.com/fund-performance which has a 14-page bibliography of articles on mutual fund performance dating back to 1984.

lviii Ferri, *The Power of Passive Investing*, p. xi.

Chapter 11: Costs Matter Far More Than You Think

lix Chapter 9, "Hidden Causes of Poor Mutual-Fund Performance" in Swensen's *Unconventional Success* gives many instructive and depressing examples of the dirty history of mutual-fund companies' search for profits at the expense of their clients.

lx Ellis, *Winning the Loser's Game*, pp. 150-151.

lxi Bogle, *Common Sense on Mutual Funds*, p. 451.

lxii Bogle, *Common Sense on Mutual Funds*, p. 25.

lxiii Research showing hedge funds' failure to add value is well documented in Larry Swedroe's *The Quest for Alpha*.

lxiv In *The Quest for Alpha*, pp. 78-79, Larry Swedroe explains how trading costs impact fund returns.

lxv Swedroe, *The Only Guide You'll Ever Need for the Right Financial Plan*, pp.63-64.

lxvi Swedroe, *The Only Guide You'll Ever Need for the Right Financial Plan*, p.64.

lxvii Robert H. Jeffrey and Robert D. Arnott, "Is Your Alpha Big Enough to Cover Its Taxes?" Journal of Portfolio Management, (Spring 1993), pp. 15-25.

lxviii Swensen, *Unconventional Success*, pp. 160-61.

lxix Cited in Rick Ferri's, *The Power of Passive Investing*, p. 111.

Chapter 12: Writing Your Investment Plan and Diversifying Your Investments

lxx In the case of REITs, valuation is a function of the price of the stock relative to the assessed value of the underlying properties the REIT owns. Thus, if an REIT company's shares are selling at, say, $12 when the assessed value of the properties it owns is $15 per share, the stock looks significantly undervalued. Of course, savvy investors may believe the property values are overstated by at least $3 per share, so one should never assume, for any given REIT, that this sort of disparity between the stock price and the assessed property value represents a bargain. Nevertheless, the time to invest in REIT funds is when they are selling at a significant discount to underlying property values (and the time to sell is when they trade at handsome premiums to underlying property values).

lxxi But if you plan to reinvest dividend payments in more shares of the fund, make sure you determine whether you will be charged for this service by the brokerage firm where you are holding your ETFs.

Chapter 13: Understanding and Managing Investment Risk

lxxii There are numerous online resources available to help investors determine how much they might safely withdraw from their savings each year in retirement. See, for example, Vanguard's retirement income website, which has articles like, "How to make your retirement savings last."

Chapter 14: How to Keep Score Properly

lxxiii Swedroe, *The Quest for Alpha*, p. 67.

lxxiv The other is Lipper Analytical Services. Morningstar is more oriented to investors, Lipper to the mutual fund industry. For example, most mutual funds report how they have performed relative to the average performance of other funds in the same category, as computed by Lipper (although it would be far more instructive if they showed performance relative to an appropriate index).

lxxv If you google "investment tracking software," you'll find articles that evaluate such programs. For example, "Pros and cons of financial tracking software programs," in *USA Today* (May 3, 2012), or Joe Lan's "The Top Portfolio Management Software," on the website of The American Association of Individual Investors.

About the Author

Until his retirement at the end of 2009, Ian Kennedy was the director of research for the global investment consulting firm, Cambridge Associates. His expertise includes endowment fund governance and management, investment planning, asset allocation, capital market history and valuation, risk management, manager selection, and benchmarking.

He now serves on the investment committee of Oxford University and the investment advisory committee of the Howard Hughes Medical Institute. He is a trustee of the James Martin Foundation, and a director of the Academy of American Poets.

His education includes a BA from Oxford and a PhD. from the University of Virginia, both in English Literature, which he taught at the University of Virginia and Bucknell University, specializing in nineteenth-century British poetry.

On his website, www.simplesmartinvesting.com, Ian gives individual investors advice on investment planning, asset allocation, risk management, manager selection, and the current market environment.

CPSIA information can be obtained at www.ICGtesting.com
Printed in the USA
LVOW01s1209060314

376250LV00006B/252/P